MICHAEL BUSSELLE'S GUIDE TO

photographing
landscapes and gardens

RotoVision

A RotoVision Book

Published and Distributed by RotoVision SA
Rue du Bugnon 7
CH-1299 Crans-Près-Céligny
Switzerland

RotoVision SA, Sales & Production Office
Sheridan House, 112/116A Western Road
Hove, East Sussex BN3 1DD, UK

Tel: +44 (0)1273 72 72 68
Fax: +44 (0)1273 72 72 69

10 9 8 7 6 5 4 3 2 1

ISBN 2-88046-676-8

Production and separations in Singapore by ProVision Pte. Ltd.
Tel:+65 334 7720
Fax:+65 334 7721

MICHAEL BUSSELLE'S GUIDE TO

photographing
landscapes and gardens

Contents

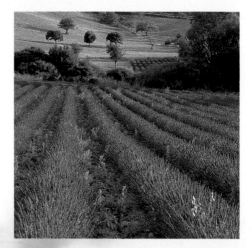

The Subject

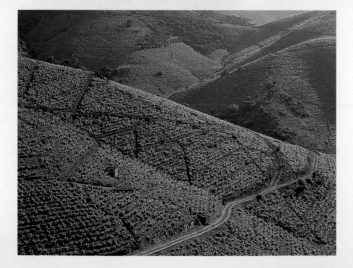

1

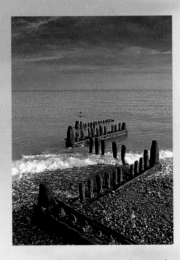

Landscape and garden photography
encompasses an enormous variety of
subjects and styles, and this chapter describes the most popular
themes and demonstrates the approach and techniques needed to
produce the most telling results.

The term landscape in the context of photography can mean a great many different things, but perhaps the most common perception is that of the classic rural view. It is most often a stunning view which makes people reach for their cameras but, paradoxically, it can be this particular type of landscape photograph which most frequently disappoints.

Seeing

I'd arrived at this location in the late afternoon of a crisp December day when the sunlight was sharp and clear, and I was immediately struck by the effect which the warm light had on the red bracken.

Thinking

I noticed that beyond there were clouds gathered over the distant mountains, casting a shadow over them. I thought that this would make an effective contrast to the well-lit foreground and accentuate the red foliage.

Acting

I climbed onto a rise in the ground, which gave me a slightly higher viewpoint and showed more of the mountains, and used a long-focus lens to frame the most colourful and interesting part of the foreground quite tightly. I used a polarising filter to maximise the colour saturation, an 81C warm-up filter to enhance the red bracken and a neutral-graduated filter to make the clouds and shadowed mountains a little darker.

Technical Details
▼ 6 x 4.5cm SLR camera with a 105–210mm zoom lens on Fuji Velvia.

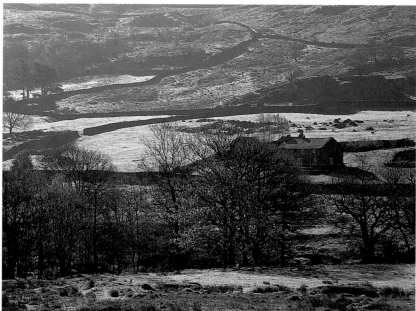

Near Tarn Howes in Cumbria, UK

The valley of the River Duddon near Ulpha in Cumbria, UK

This springtime shot, taken in the early morning, appealed to me because the back lighting had created an almost monochromatic effect. I used a long-focus lens to isolate a small area of the scene, which has accentuated the textural quality of the newly emerging leaves and bare branches of the trees.

Technical Details

6 x 4.5cm SLR camera with a 105–210mm zoom lens, polarising, 81C warm-up and neutral-graduated filters on Fuji Velvia.

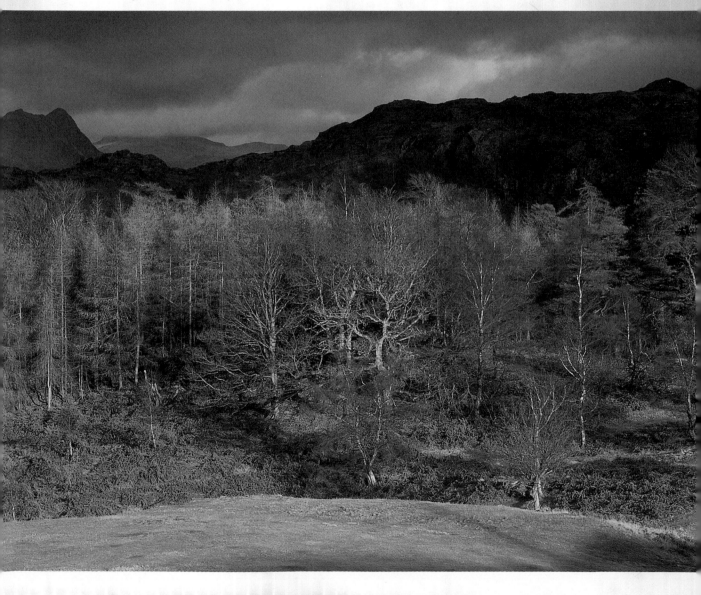

Seeing

It was initially the striking effect of the bare-branched trees silhouetted against a dramatically cloudy sky which attracted Julien Busselle to this scene.

Thinking

He felt that more was needed to make a satisfying composition and found a viewpoint from where the small group of back-lit sheep provided an ideal focus in the foreground.

Acting

Julien framed the shot so the two trees created a frame around the image, along with the shadowed hillock in the immediate foreground, and so they were most effectively placed against the sky. This has helped to concentrate attention on the main focus of interest. He used an 81C warm-up filter to make the colour of the brown grass slightly richer and a neutral-graduated filter to darken the top area of the sky.

Technical Details
6 x 4.5cm SLR camera with a 55–110mm zoom lens on Fuji Velvia.

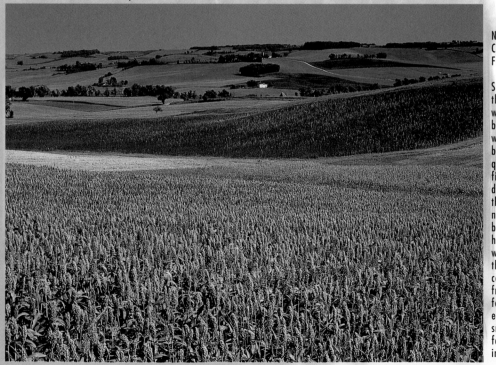

Near the town of Condom in Gascony, France

Shot in the autumn in the middle of the day, when there was a clear blue sky, this scene was rather blandly lit but the strong textural quality of the millet field and the distant dead sunflowers gave the image the necessary degree of bite. I used the highlighted white-walled farmhouse as the focus for the composition, and framed the shot so the foreground was emphasised and only a small strip of the featureless sky was included.

Technique

Always look at the possibility of including **foreground details** when shooting distant views, as this can help to create a feeling of depth and distance in the image as well as adding an element of interest to the composition.

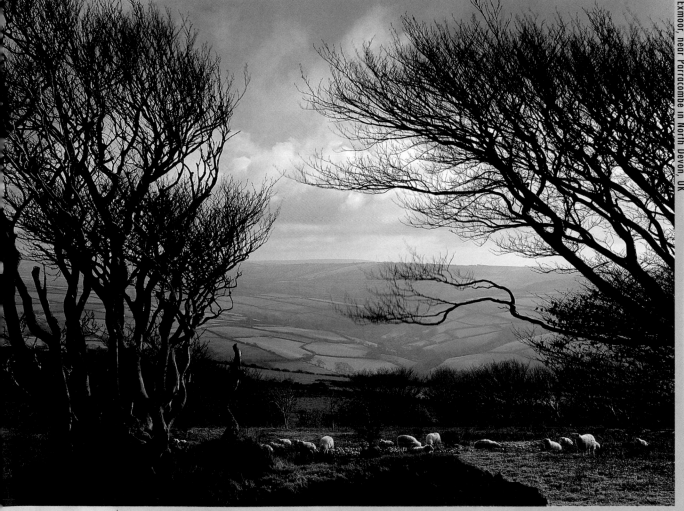

Exmoor, near Parracombe in North Devon, UK

Technical Details

6 x 4.5cm SLR camera with a 55–110mm zoom lens, 81C warm-up and neutral-graduated filters on Fuji Velvia.

The Coast

There is something quite magical about the place where the land meets the sea and as a location for landscape photography it offers an immense variety of possibilities. From broad vistas of the coastline itself to abstract details of rocks and sand, a perceptive photographer will seldom be short of inspiration.

Seeing

It was late in the afternoon of what had been a largely overcast winter's day when I arrived at this spot. The sun had just begun to emerge through a gap in the clouds and the late hour gave it a very pleasing warm quality.

Thinking

The sunlight was also glancing from the fence rail on the left of the path and creating an attractive highlight. I felt the path and fence rail would make an effective foreground and at the same time lead the eye towards the sea, which was intended to be the main feature of the shot.

Acting

I chose a viewpoint which allowed me to include enough of the path and fence to establish them but also included a large area of the sky and sea. I needed to use a very wide-angle lens to frame the image in the way I wanted and used a neutral-graduated filter to prevent the sky from overexposing.

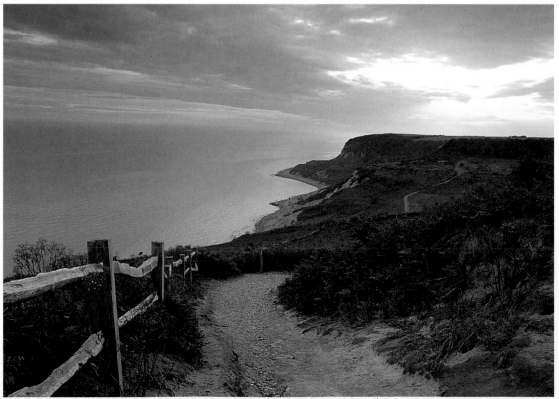

Fairlight Cove near Hastings in East Sussex, UK

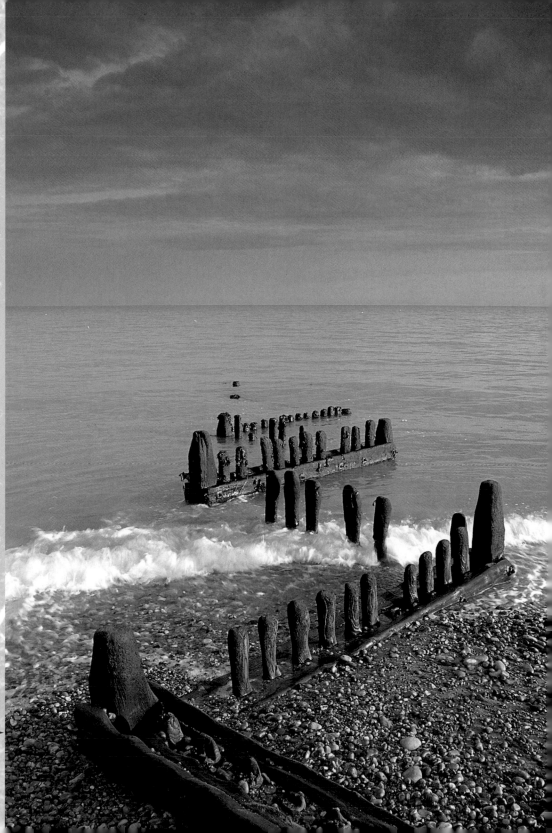

Winchelsea Beach near Rye in East Sussex, UK

The zigzag line created by this eroded groyne was the inspiration for this shot, taken on the same afternoon as the other image on this spread. I used the upright format to allow the inclusion of a generous area of sky and framed the shot so the sky, sea and beach occupied about equal portions of the image. I used an 81C warm-up filter to accentuate the warm quality of the afternoon light, a polarising filter to enrich the colour of the sea and a neutral-graduated filter to darken the sky a little.

Technical Details
35mm SLR camera with a 20–35mm zoom lens, 81C warm-up and neutral-graduated filters on Fuji Velvia.

Technical Details
35mm SLR camera with a 20–35mm zoom lens, 81C warm-up, neutral-graduated and polarising filters on Fuji Velvia.

Seeing

It had been cloudy all day and I was returning, without a photograph in the bag, to my hotel when I saw this scene in my rear-view mirror as I drove along the coast road.

Thinking

I needed to find somewhere I could stop quickly on this busy road and also a place where I could have an uninterrupted view of the coastline. A lay-by appeared as if by divine intervention and I quickly set up the camera and framed the shot roughly.

Acting

The clouds were moving swiftly and the breaks between them caused beams of sunlight to flicker though with varying degrees of brightness. I decided to use a neutral-graduated filter as, most of the time, I felt that the brightest part of the sky would be considerably overexposed in relation to the sea. I made a number of exposures, all with quite different effects, over a period of ten minutes or so when the breaks gave way to solid cloud again.

Technical Details

▼ 35mm SLR camera with a 35–70mm zoom lens, neutral-graduated and 81C warm-up filters on Fuji Velvia.

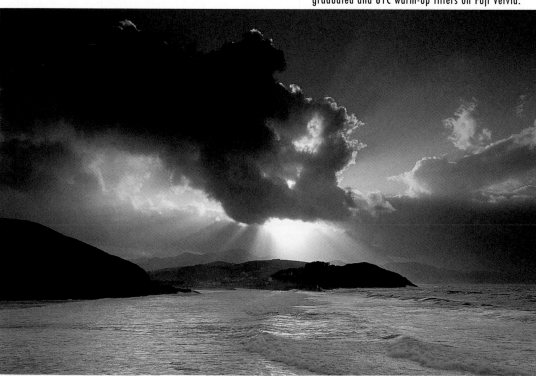

Near San Sebastian in the Basque region of Spain

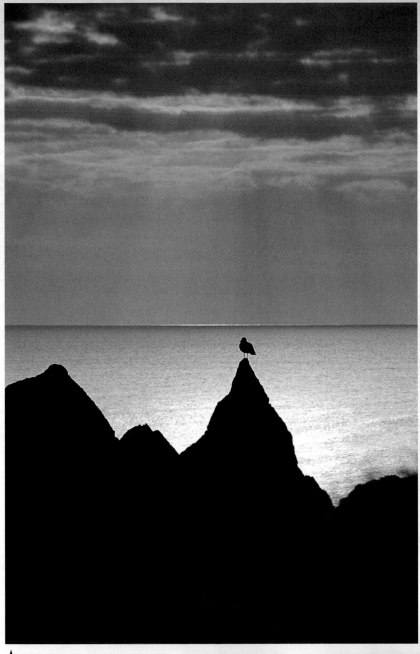

Hartland Quay, North Devon, UK

Julien Busselle spotted this perfectly posed seagull as he was setting up his camera to shoot a seascape. He quickly switched to a long focus lens and framed the image so that the horizon line divided the image in two and the seagull was almost exactly in the centre. He used a neutral-graduated filter to darken the top of the sky and gave one stop extra exposure than indicated to allow for the brightly lit sea, bracketing half a stop each side.

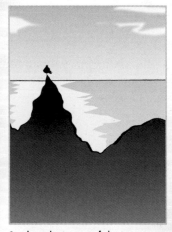

See how the impact of the image would have been lessened by framing the shot with the seagull placed on the intersection of thirds.

▲ Technical Details

35mm SLR camera with a 75–300mm zoom lens and a neutral-graduated filter on Fuji Velvia.

Mountains & Uplands

For landscape images with a more dramatic quality, the steep contours and rugged nature of mountain scenery offers enormous potential, providing images with strong textures and a rich range of tones. Not only is the landscape itself very different in both appearance and mood but its very nature can also provide the photographer with unusual and less familiar viewpoints.

Seeing

In early spring, the fresh green vine leaves create a powerful colour and the monochromatic effect heightens the pattern of the hillsides.

Thinking

I was shooting towards the light and the sky was hazy, creating a blank, featureless tone. I needed to find an additional feature or detail to give the image a focus of attention.

Acting

By driving a little further up the mountain road, I found that I was able to place this small path and stone hut at the bottom of the frame in a way which allowed me to use a long-focus lens to emphasise them, as well as eliminating the sky. I used a polarising filter to increase the colour saturation and an 81C warm-up filter to enrich the green foliage.

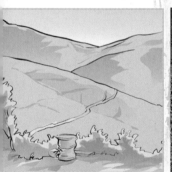

A wider view of the scene, showing more of the sky and foreground, would have been far less effective.

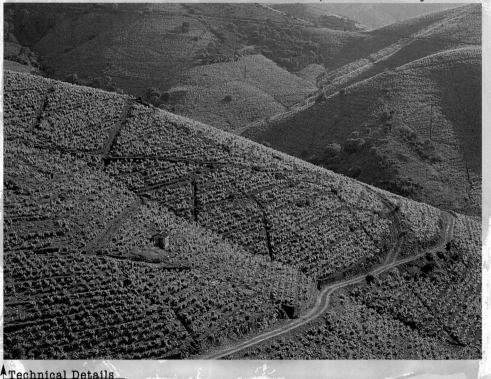

Near Banyuls in the Roussillon region of France

Technical Details
6 x 4.5cm SLR camera with a 55–110mm zoom lens, 81C warm-up, neutral-graduated and polarising filters on Fuji Velvia.

Near Torla in the Ordesa National Park in Huesca, Spain

The lighting in this scene created a rich range of tones and the sparkle on the river and highlighted sheep provided a strong focus of attention. I used a polarising filter to increase the colour saturation, and to subdue the highlights on the water, an 81C warm-up filter to eliminate a potential blue cast and a neutral-graduated filter to darken the top area of the sky.

Rule of Thumb

As on the coast, the light at high altitudes has a strong presence of ultraviolet light and warm-up filters are often essential to overcome potential blue casts. Atmospheric haze can also be a problem in the mountains and a polarising filter will help to give greater clarity in distant views.

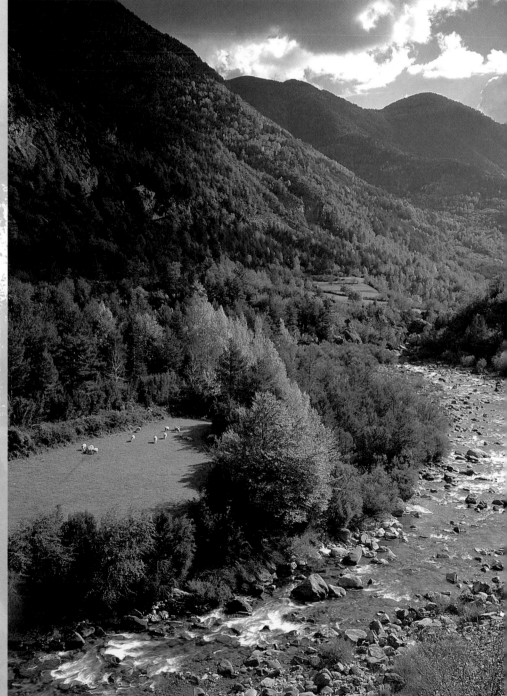

Seeing

I had been travelling along a small valley and as the sun had disappeared some while before I assumed that my photography for the day was over. As I turned the corner I saw that a lingering shaft of sunlight had created this striking red tip on the snow-covered mountain top.

Thinking

I had to find a viewpoint, stop and set up very quickly as I could see that the effect would last for only a moment.

Acting

I was very lucky to find a track which led up onto a small terrace – the village rubbish dump, in fact – and managed to shoot two or three frames before the sunlight was extinguished. I used a long-focus lens to isolate a small area of the distant scene and underexposed by about two-thirds of a stop to increase the saturation of the red-tinted snow and to make the blue-shaded mountains a darker tone than appeared visually.

The Massif des Ecrins near Grenoble in the Isere region of France

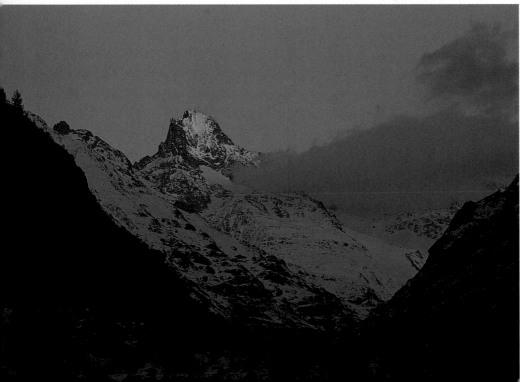

Technique

It's quite probable that you will find viewpoints from where there is a potentially good photograph but that the sun is in the wrong position. Reconnaissance can be a very useful part of landscape photography and you should develop the habit of making a note of such locations on your map. I mark them with a highlight pen and use a compass to calculate when the best time to return might be.

Technical Details
6 x 4.5cm SLR camera with a 105–210mm zoom lens on Fuji Velvia.

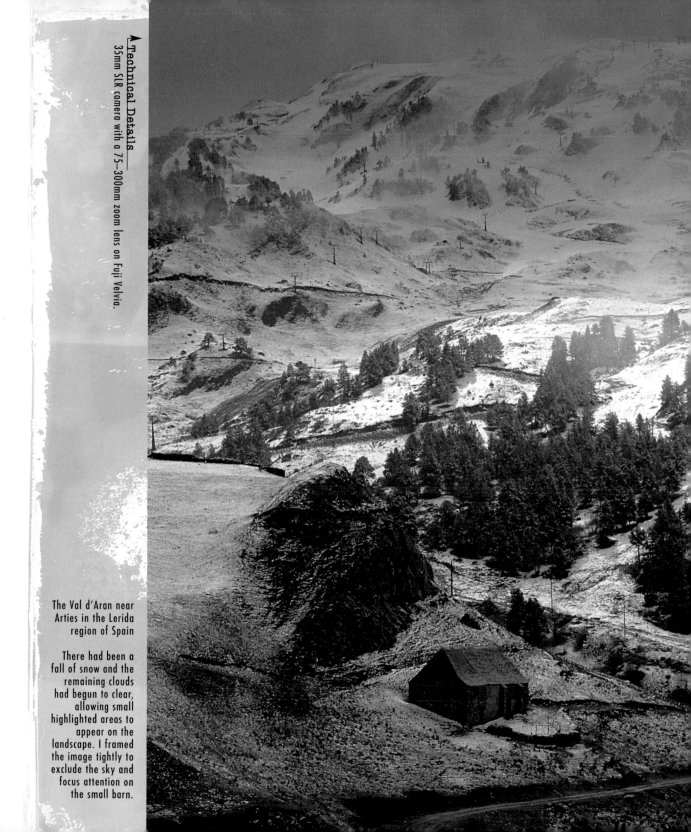

▲ Technical Details
35mm SLR camera with a 75–300mm zoom lens on Fuji Velvia.

The Val d'Aran near Arties in the Lerida region of Spain

There had been a fall of snow and the remaining clouds had begun to clear, allowing small highlighted areas to appear on the landscape. I framed the image tightly to exclude the sky and focus attention on the small barn.

What the flatter countryside
of heath, marsh and moorland may lack in terms of dramatic contours it can often make up for
with its moods of mystery and solitude. It's a landscape in which you need to look carefully for
good viewpoints and make use of foreground interest
as well as being aware of the effects which can be
created by atmospheric lighting.

Seeing

It was midwinter when I saw this scene and was attracted by the subdued colours and rich textures of the dead grass and heather. I also like the swirly effect of the wintry clouds and the hint of colour in them created by the low angle of the sun.

Thinking

I felt that some foreground interest would give another element and a feeling of depth to the picture and found this cluster of rocks did the trick, while the inclusion of a small part of the curving road created a useful focus of interest.

Acting

I chose a viewpoint quite close to the rocks to accentuate the perspective effect and also to hide some of the road, which I didn't want to be too dominant. I used a wide-angle lens to frame the image, an 81B warm-up filter to eliminate the possibility of a blue cast and a neutral-graduated filter to make the tone and colour of the sky a little richer.

Technical Details
▼ 6 x 4.5cm SLR camera with a 55–110mm zoom lens,
81B warm-up and neutral-graduated filters on Fuji Velvia.

The moors near Askrigg in the Yorkshire Dales, UK

Dartmoor in South
Devon, UK

Late afternoon sunlight
had created a very
pleasing colour and
texture on this group of
rocks, a small Tor. I
framed the image quite
tightly as I wanted to
emphasise the very
attractive quality of
light on the rocks and
much of the rest of the
scene was in shadow. I
used a neutral-
graduated filter to
darken the top area of
the sky and an 81B
warm-up filter to
accentuate the effect of
the warm light.

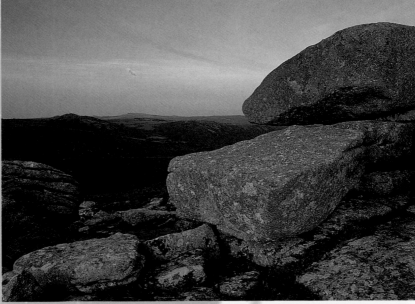

Technical Details
▼ 6 x 4.5cm SLR camera with a 50mm wide-angle lens, 81B warm-up and neutral-graduated filters on Fuji Velvia.

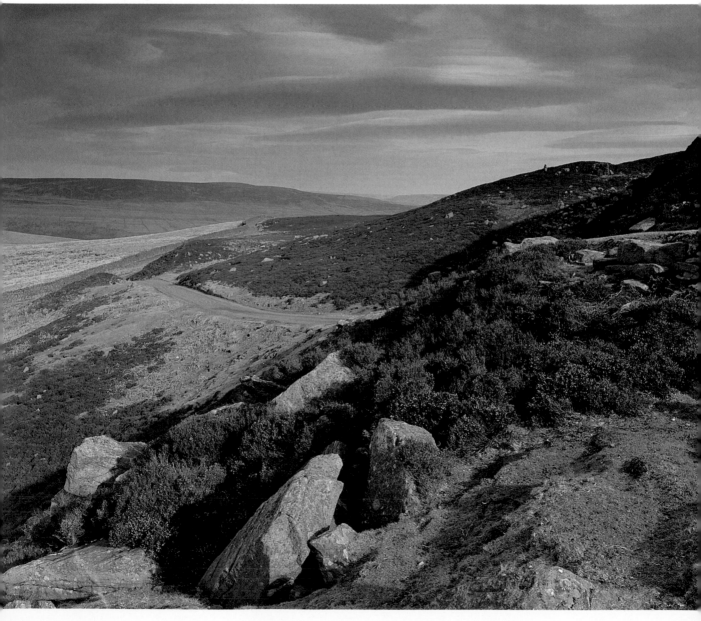

Rule of Thumb

A higher than average viewpoint can often produce a more effective composition, especially when the landscape is fairly flat. It can sometimes be enough just to find a slight rise in the ground but some professional landscape photographers carry a small, lightweight stepladder and a tall tripod.

Technique

When shooting **sunset pictures** where the sun, or an area of very bright sky, is included in the frame it is best to take an **exposure reading** from the area just above or to the side of it to avoid the risk of underexposure.

Rule of Thumb

The less you include in an image the more impact it is likely to have. Many disappointing photographs would have been improved if the photographer had taken two or more photographs instead of trying to include all of the scene in one image.

Technical Details
▼ 6 x 4.5cm SLR camera with a 105–210mm zoom lens on Fuji Velvia.

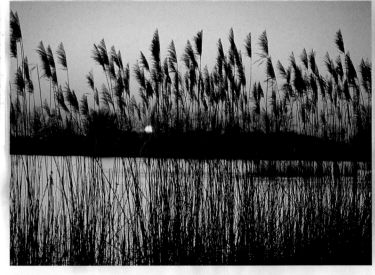

The Dombes region near Bourg-en-Bresse, France

Although this is a very appealing and atmospheric region, it is, nevertheless, rather flat and featureless and its main attractions are the numerous reed-fringed lakes. I shot this scene in winter and used the fairly weak setting sun as the main focus of interest, and the row of reeds as a decorative foreground, shooting on a long-focus lens to minimise the effect of perspective and to give the image a strong graphic quality.

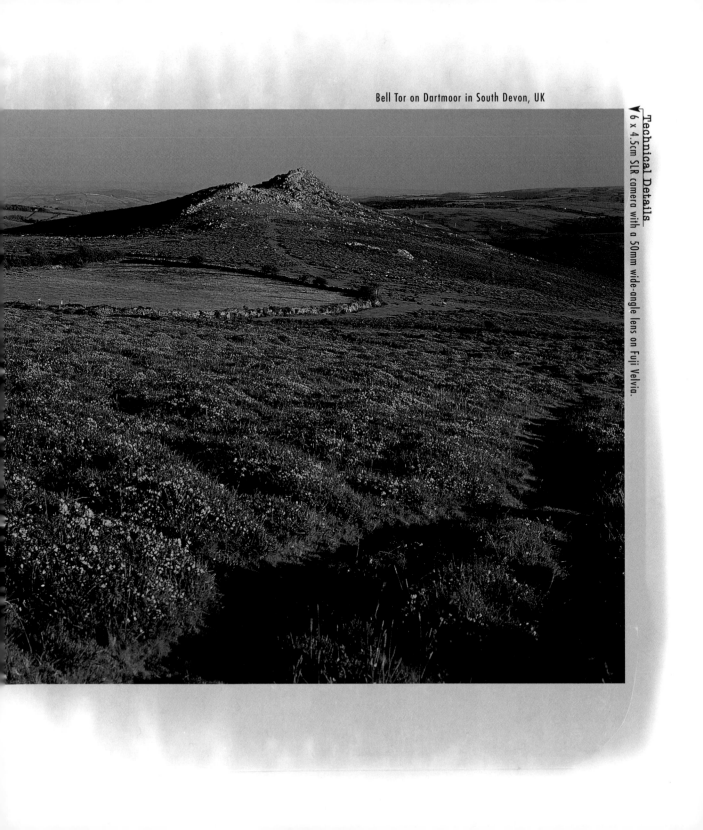

Bell Tor on Dartmoor in South Devon, UK

Technical Details. 6 x 4.5cm SLR camera with a 50mm wide-angle lens on Fuji Velvia.

Lakes, Rivers & Waterfalls

Whether dark and mysterious or pale turquoise and crystal clear, whether rushing or motionless, sparkling or turgid, water, in all its natural forms, has a constantly changing appearance which offers considerable photographic potential. The presence of water in a landscape photograph can not only add an element of interest and atmosphere to an image but it can also increase the contrast and add sparkle to a scene on a hazy or overcast day, when the lighting may otherwise be too soft for a successful photograph.

Seeing

I had travelled around this lake during the day looking for pictures but it's a rather featureless expanse of water and I felt my best chance of an interesting image was when the sun set or at dusk. For this reason I was keen to find some details or objects which would make an interesting foreground when I saw this partially submerged tree.

Thinking

I decided to return at the end of the day with the intention of shooting at sunset. In fact I did so, and it was quite spectacular, but I waited for half an hour or so afterwards to find that the sky produced this more subtle and very appealing pinky blue hue which was nicely reflected in the still water.

Acting

I chose a viewpoint which placed the most attractive area of the sky behind the tree and framed the image so there was only a small strip of shore visible and the tree was quite large in the viewfinder.

Technical Details

▼ 35mm SLR camera with a 35–70mm zoom lens, 81C warm-up and neutral-graduated filters on Fuji Velvia.

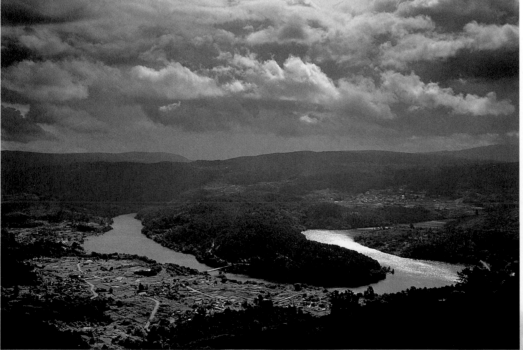

The River Mino near Pontevedra in Galicia, Spain

This was, as you can see, a very cloudy, overcast day but as I drove up out of the river valley this break in the cloud occurred, allowing a small spotlight of sunshine to play on the river. It provided a vital element of contrast for this shot, without which the image would have been flat and uninteresting. I used a neutral-graduated filter to prevent the bright parts of the sky from overexposing.

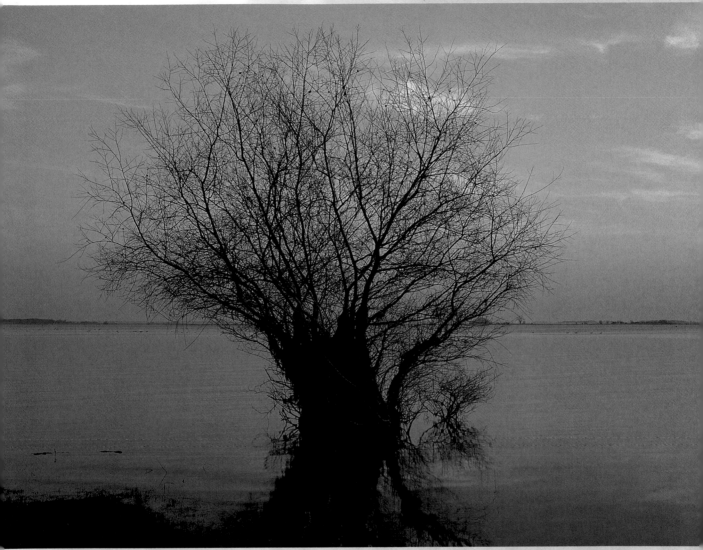

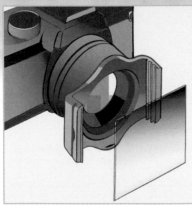

▲ Technical Details
6 x 4.5cm SLR camera with a
55–110mm zoom lens on Fuji Velvia.

Square filter systems are more
practical and controllable than
screw-on versions. Here a square
filter holder secures a neutral-
graduated filter.

Rule of Thumb

A polarising filter can be especially
useful when photographing still water
as it can often help to increase the
strength of reflections of the sky or
surrounding details. It is also very
effective in controlling the brightness
of highlights created on back-lit water.

Seeing

It was a dull, overcast winter's day when I visited this valley – in fact, it was raining and I had been unable to find any suitable subjects so far. But this waterfall had a very attractive quality in the soft light and the water was flowing quite fast.

Thinking

It was a classic situation for the slow-shutter-speed technique as I was sure that the moving water combined with the soft lighting would create a particularly nice effect.

Acting

I chose a viewpoint and framed my shot so that the water created a Y shape in the rocks and appeared to flow directly towards the camera and, at the same time, excluded all extraneous details. I used a polarising filter and a small aperture which allowed me to use an exposure of several seconds.

Technical Details
▼ 6 x 4.5cm SLR camera with a 105–210mm zoom lens on Fuji Velvia.

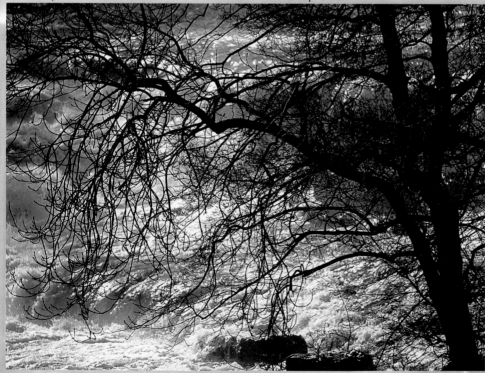

The Aysgarth Falls in the Yorkshire Dales, UK

This was taken in midwinter and the river was in full flood, along with many others in the region. I liked the monochromatic effect created by the back-lighting and decided to use a long-focus lens to limit the image to the most dramatic section of the cascading water, using just part of the foreground tree as a sort of frame. I set a fast shutter speed to record the water with a degree of texture.

Technical Details →
6 x 4.5cm SLR camera with a 105–210mm zoom lens, 81B warm-up and polarising filters on Fuji Velvia.

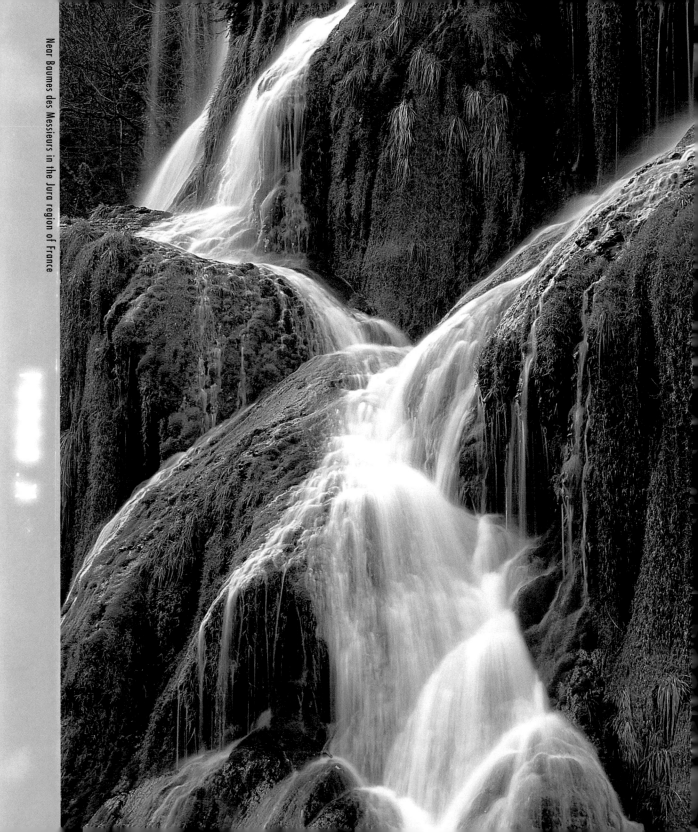
Near Baumes des Messieurs in the Jura region of France

The tree is a crucial element in landscape photography for a number of reasons. Landscape images tend to be dominated by essentially horizontal lines — those of the contours of the land and the horizon — and the vertical line created by a tree often provides both an arresting element of contrast and a powerful focus of attention. Woods and forests also have enormous pictorial potential when viewed both as a broad vista and when seen as a source of closer images in which elements like shape, texture and pattern can be exploited to the full.

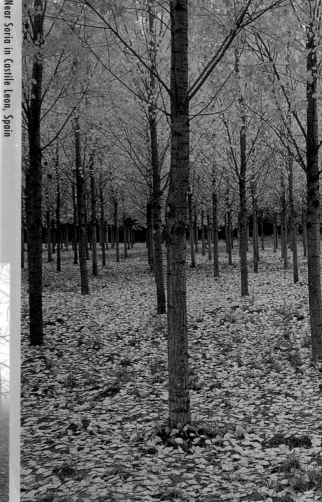

Near Soria in Castile Leon, Spain

Seeing

It was late evening, on what had been an overcast day, when I saw this plantation of young poplar trees. The light level was very low and this seemed to give the autumnal foliage an almost fluorescent glow.

Thinking

I decided that the most effective image would be produced by emphasising the element of pattern which was created by the orderly planting and realised this would be further accentuated by the monochromatic quality of the image.

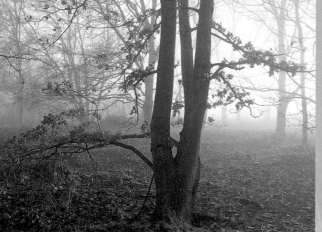

Seal Chart Woods near Sevenoaks in Kent, UK

A misty day can be perfect for woodland photography because it simplifies the image and masks unwanted background details. I used a close viewpoint and framed this tree quite tightly to ensure the tree stood out clearly from the misty background and used an 81B warm-up filter to eliminate a potential blue cast and to emphasise the autumnal colours.

◄ **Technical Details**
6 x 4.5cm SLR camera with a 55–110mm zoom lens and an 81B warm-up filter on Fuji Velvia.

35mm SLR camera with a 35mm perspective-control lens on Fuji Velvia.

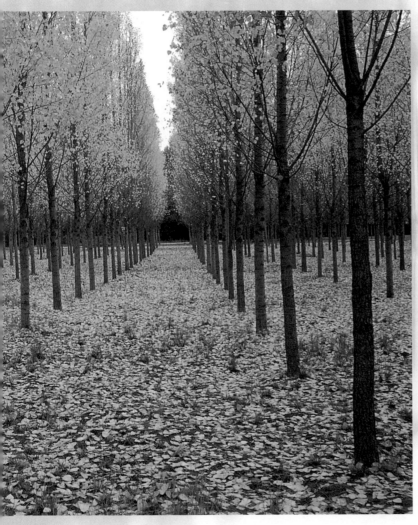

This diagram shows how the tree trunks would have appeared to converge had the camera been tilted down instead of using a shift lens.

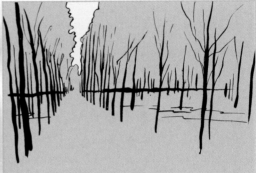

Acting

The only feasible viewpoint was from the roadside bank which was at a higher level than the floor of the plantation. I felt it was vital to retain the parallel tree trunks but I also needed to include the base of the nearest trees, which would have meant tilting the camera down and creating converging verticals so I used my **perspective-control lens** to overcome this. I used a **small aperture** to obtain **maximum depth of field**.

Rule of Thumb

The photographic possibilities provided by trees, both individually and collectively, are often at their greatest in the winter months when the absence of foliage reveals the intricate shapes and patterns of bare branches.

Trees & Forests

Seeing

It was actually raining when I saw this scene and the light was very poor. These lighting conditions often intensify colours like this autumnal foliage and can be far more effective than a bright sunny day.

Thinking

I felt I needed to frame the image quite tightly so that the colour and the pattern created by the leaves in the foreground would be emphasised.

Acting

My viewpoint was from the far bank of the small lake and I needed to use a long-focus lens to compose the image in the way I wanted. I found that the addition of a polarising filter and an 81C warm-up filter produced a dramatic increase in the richness and saturation of the autumn colour.

Technique

To take a series of photographs of a specific tree, or group of trees, from the same viewpoint at intervals through the course of a year can be a very satisfying and fascinating way of building a collection of photographs.

Technical Details
▼ 6 x 4.5cm SLR camera with a 55–110mm zoom lens on Fuji Velvia.

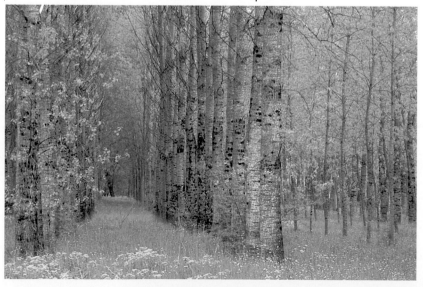

Near Cognac in the Charente region of France

It was the essentially monochromatic quality of the fresh green spring foliage which appealed to me in this scene as I drove through the valley of the River Charente. The pattern created by the tree trunks was also a powerful element in the composition and these two qualities enhanced each other. I used a long-focus lens to isolate a small area of the scene from a quite distant viewpoint.

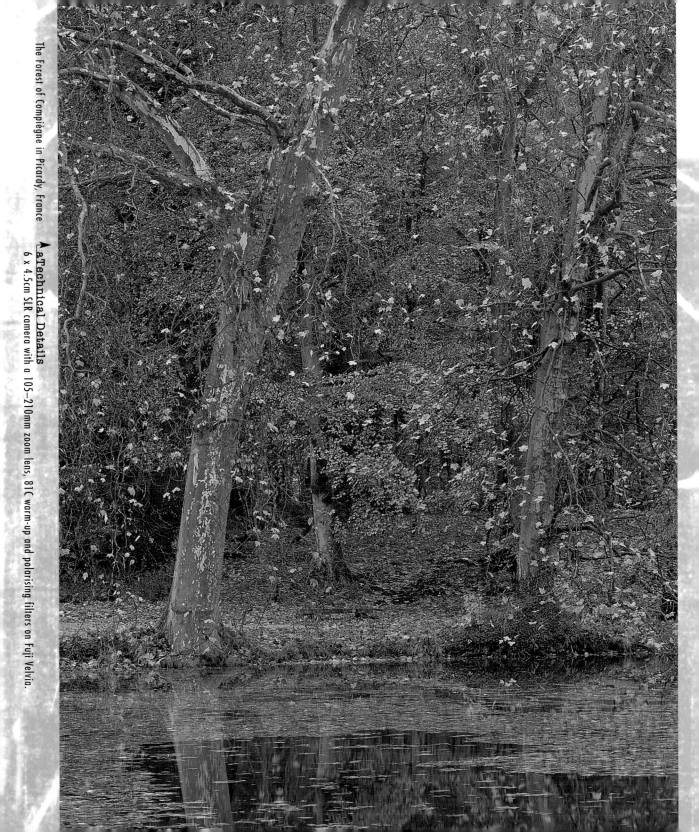

The Forest of Compiègne in Picardy, France

▲ a Technical Details
6 x 4.5cm SLR camera with a 105–210mm zoom lens, 81C warm-up and polarising filters on Fuji Velvia.

The Urban Landscape

To many people, landscape photography means the great outdoors and the appeal of the open countryside. But, if only from a purely photographic point of view, it can make a refreshing change to look for photographs among the angular forms of buildings instead of the softer contours of the land. Many cities are a fascinating mix of weathered ancient buildings and gleaming new constructions of stainless steel, glass and concrete, and the contrast can be both inspiring and stimulating, especially for those who are more accustomed to photographing the rural scene.

Seeing

It was quite a bleak, wintry day when I visited the Louvre and at first the possibility of an interesting shot of the famous glass pyramid seemed unlikely. But as I walked around it I found that by looking back towards the brightest part of the sky, a quite striking degree of relief was created along with some pleasingly soft and subtle colours.

Thinking

I felt that to shoot the pyramid alone might not produce an image with enough contrast and so I looked for a way of introducing a darker foreground.

Acting

I walked to the far side of the pool behind me and found that from there I could include some of the water in the foreground along with part of the fountain and as these were both in shadow they provided an effective darker-toned frame to the image of the pyramid. Then all I had to do was wait for a gap in the stream of people passing between the pool and the pyramid.

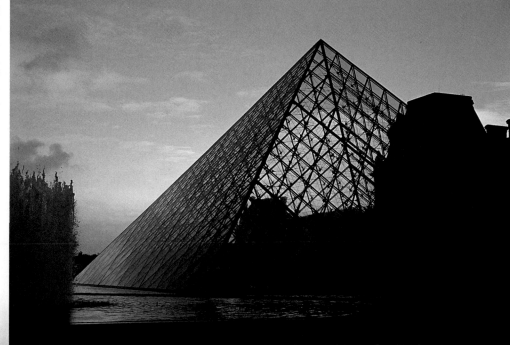

Technical Details
35mm SLR camera with a 24–85mm zoom lens and an 81B warm-up filter on Kodak Ektachrome SW.

The courtyard of the Louvre Museum in Paris, France

San Francisco, USA

I found this viewpoint of the typically steep streets of this city and although it was a day on which the lighting was not ideal, from here the sun was glancing off some of the buildings, giving the scene a rather surreal quality. I decided to use a long-focus lens to frame the most strongly-lit part of the image and refrained from using a warm-up filter so the image would have this curious blue-grey quality.

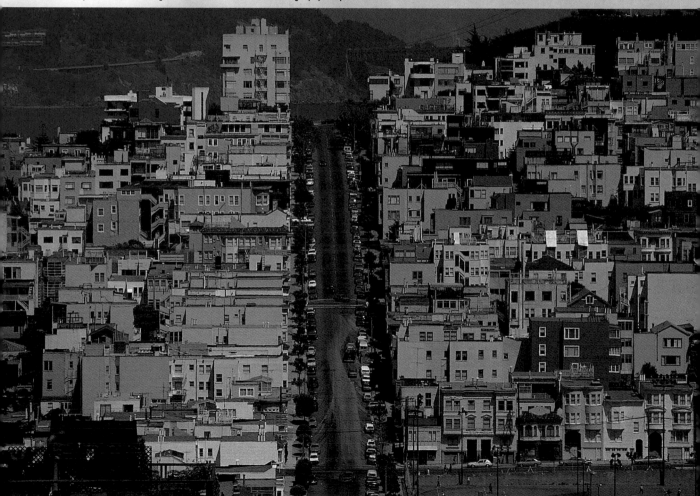

Technical Details

35mm SLR camera with a 200mm lens on Kodachrome 64.

Seeing

This steel and glass building, like many others, has much photographic potential, but I wanted to avoid the more obvious shot of its façade so I walked around and inside the complex looking for a viewpoint which would give me a rather more ambiguous image of the structure.

Thinking

I liked this viewpoint which enabled me to use this exterior lift shaft and archway as a foreground and frame for the more distant building.

Acting

I needed to use a wide-angle lens to frame the image in the way I wanted while still including enough of the structure. I calculated my exposure so that the foreground details were silhouetted and waited until the lift and some passengers reached the ideal point in the frame before shooting.

Technical Details
▼ 6 x 4.5cm SLR camera with a 20–35mm zoom lens on Fuji Velvia.

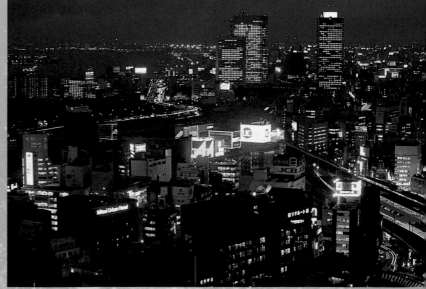

Tokyo, Japan

I shot this image from a high-rise building through a window by placing the camera lens as close to the glass as possible. I waited until I felt that the scene had become dark enough to allow the illuminated buildings to record quite brightly but before the sky became completely black.

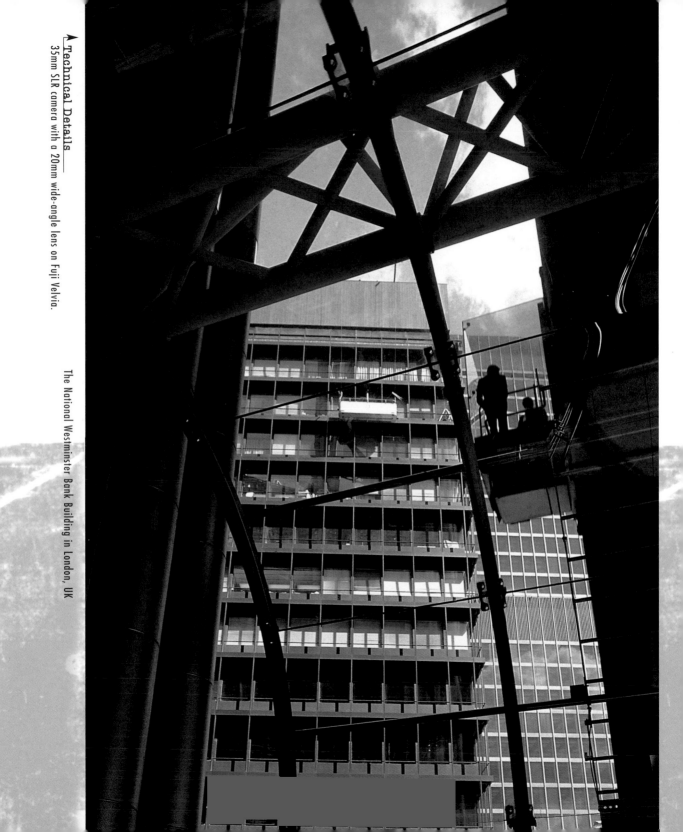

Technical Details
35mm SLR camera with a 20mm wide-angle lens on Fuji Velvia.

The National Westminster Bank Building in London, UK

Borders & Shrubs

The planting of borders and the distribution of flowering shrubs are what give a garden its basic structure and colour. Garden design is a skilled art and it's often only a question of careful choice of viewpoint and framing to ensure satisfying pictures with a good sense of design and colour.

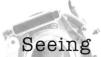

Seeing

The circular borders planted with pansies around the fruit trees were a striking feature of this lawned area. Finding a suitable viewpoint was difficult as they were widely spaced and my initial attempts resulted in too much lawn and not enough colour.

Thinking

I decided to select just one island border and use a distant viewpoint and long-focus lens to compress the colour and shapes it contained.

Acting

This viewpoint allowed me to place the distant garden wall behind the tree which, together with the small area of grass, helped to contain the image and provide an uncluttered background. I framed the image very tightly, partly to concentrate attention on the contrasting colours of the flowers but also to crop out the blank sky above the wall. It was a very dull, overcast day which provided an ideal light for the colour subject, but the inclusion of white sky would have destroyed the image's impact.

Powerscourt Gardens near Wicklow in County Wicklow, Eire

Rule of Thumb

It's best to resist the temptation to shoot your pictures right away, as the viewpoint you first see is not always the best and it pays to explore all the possibilities first.

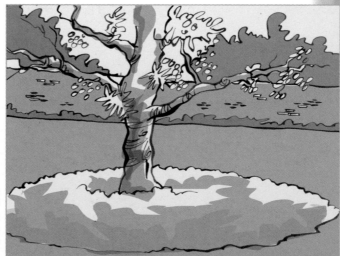

See how much less effective a wider view of the scene would have been and how distracting the top of the wall and blank sky would have looked.

Technical Details
6 x 4.5cm SLR camera with a 105–210mm zoom lens and an 81B warm-up filter on Fuji Velvia.

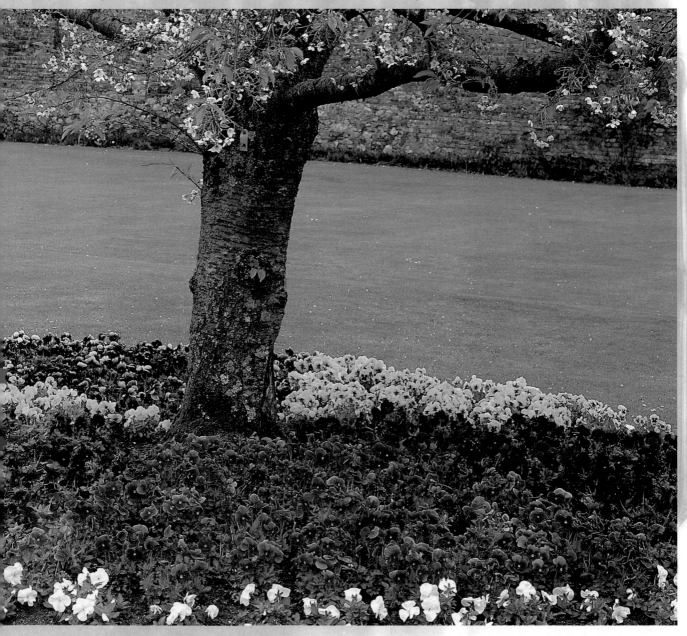

Borders & Shrubs

Technical Details
▼ 6 x 4.5cm SLR camera with a 105–210mm zoom lens, polarising and 81B warm-up filters on Fuji Velvia.

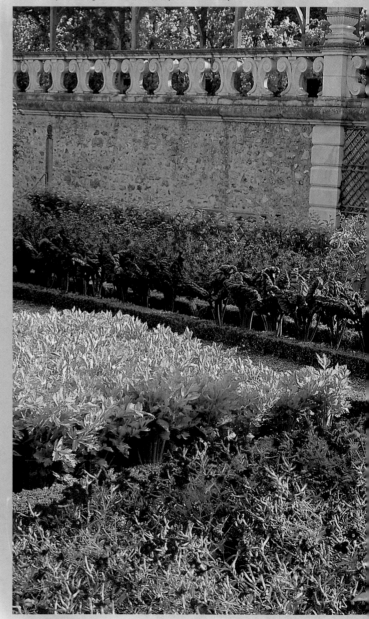

Seeing

A striking **feature** of these gardens is the unusual creative planting which combines flowers with vegetables. This section of the garden caught my eye because the red blooms of the nicotiana and scarlet stems of the chard created an eye-catching zigzag.

Thinking

I chose a **viewpoint** from where this effect was most noticeable and which placed the **ornamental** wall at the top of the image.

Acting

I used a **long-focus** lens to isolate a small section of the scene, emphasising the zigzag, and to crop out distracting details above the wall. I used a polarising filter to enhance the colour saturation and a warm-up filter to give the reds an added boost. I selected a small aperture to ensure the image was **sharp** from foreground to background.

Rule of Thumb

It's very tempting when you see colourful borders or arrangements of shrubs to photograph them as they appear to the eye. But this can produce very disappointing results as we see things in a very selective way, focusing our attention only upon what interests us in a scene and ignoring other details. When taking photographs it's necessary to impose this selectivity in the way you frame and compose your shots if you are to avoid muddled and uncohesive images.

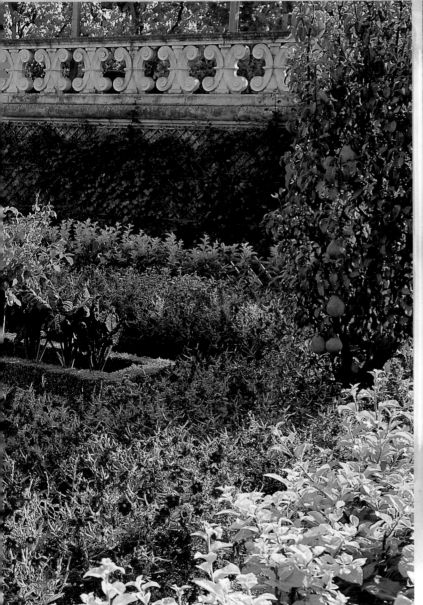

The gardens of Chateau Villandry near Tours in the Loire Valley, France

Technical Details
▼ 35mm SLR camera with a 20–35mm zoom lens, polarising and 81B warm-up filters on Fuji Velvia.

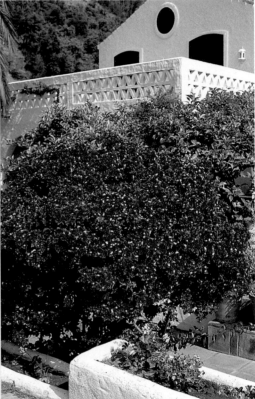

A villa near Estepona in Andalucía, Spain

The vivid colour of this bougainvillea in full bloom needed a fairly neutral contrasting background, so I found a viewpoint which enabled me to place the white wall of the villa behind the vine. I used a warm-up filter because the colour quality of the midday summer sunlight was quite blue, and a polarising filter to increase the colour saturation of the blooms.

Garden Landscapes

A garden is a man-made landscape and, as such, it offers the photographer the great advantage of having been consciously constructed with composition in mind. Unlike conventional landscapes, where the beauty of the countryside can be marred by man-made intrusions, a garden can be beautiful because of them.

Seeing

The first colours of the autumn foliage were beginning to appear on this visit to the garden, and the effect of this red-leafed tree was quite dramatic in contrast to the still-green trees around it. The light was also sparklingly clear, which gave the scene a wonderful clarity.

Thinking

I wanted to use the tree as a focus of attention in a wider view of the garden and chose this viewpoint close to the edge of a small lake where it would create some interest in the foreground. The sky, too, was very attractive – a good, clear blue with dense white clouds.

Acting

I framed my shot and tilted the camera upwards so that most of the large white cloud which had appeared was included and the tree was placed on a line about one-third from the bottom of the frame. I used the widest setting on my zoom lens to accommodate a little of the water and the reflections in the foreground and angled the camera so the tree was slightly off-centre. I used a polarising filter to make the sky a richer blue and give the cloud greater relief, and a warm-up filter to emphasise the rich colour of the foliage.

Rule of Thumb

It's important to find an object, colour or tone within a landscape picture which can act as a centre of interest around which the other details of the image can be balanced.

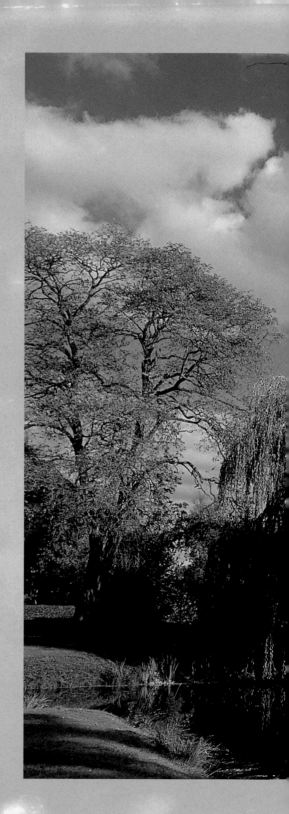

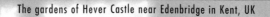

The gardens of Hever Castle near Edenbridge in Kent, UK

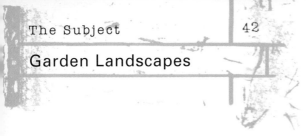

Technical Details
▼ 6 x 4.5cm SLR camera with a 55–110mm zoom lens,
polarising and 81B warm-up filters on Fuji Velvia.

Mount Ushmore Gardens near Wicklow in County Wicklow, Eire

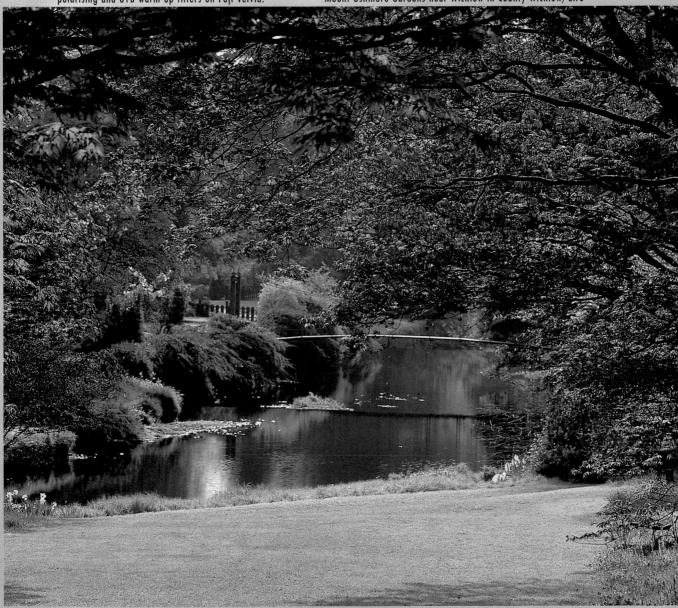

Rule of Thumb

The inclusion of foreground interest when shooting a distant scene can be a very effective way of creating a sense of depth and distance in an image, but you will need to use a small aperture if you want both close and distant details to be sharp.

Seeing

It was the rich colour of the acer foliage which attracted me to this scene, contrasted against the soft spring green of the grass beyond.

Thinking

The effect of the leaf colour was strongest when viewed against the light so I looked for a viewpoint which would enable me to capture this and where I would also be close enough to the tree to make it the dominant colour. I also wanted to find a way of excluding the rather pale, milky sky which would have diluted the effect of the rich colours.

Acting

This viewpoint achieved my aims but I needed to use a wide-angle lens to include as much of the tree as possible. I found that a polarising filter had a dramatic effect on the red leaves, making them much richer, and I used an 81B warm-up filter to emphasise the reds and greens even more.

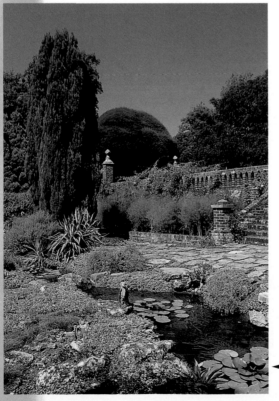

Doddington Manor Gardens near Ashford, in Kent, UK

I used the camera in upright format with a wide-angle lens for this shot, as I wanted to include both the pond in the foreground and the tall tree in the background. I used a polarising filter to make the sky a deeper blue and increase the colour saturation of the foliage and an 81EF warm-up filter as the blue sky and midday summer sunlight would have otherwise created a blue cast.

Technical Details

35mm SLR camera with a 20–35mm zoom lens, polarising and 81EF warm-up filters on Fuji Velvia.

Gardens are usually designed to complement a
house, and even when they are quite separate they
often have architectural features which are incorporated into their design.
Including buildings in garden photographs can frequently provide an interesting
element of both contrast and scale.

Seeing

This was a day of beautiful summer sunlight which was
illuminating the front of the house perfectly. But it was also quite
harsh and contrasty and created an unpleasant effect on
the roses and lavender in front of it.

Fitz House in the village of
Teffont Evias in Wiltshire, UK

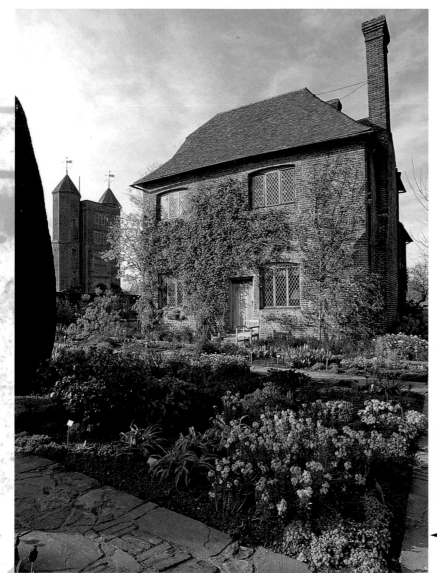

Sissinghurst Castle Gardens near Tenterden in Kent, UK

I used a wide-angle shift lens to photograph this cottage as the viewpoint was quite restricted and I wanted to include both the flower border in the foreground and the top of the tall chimney without having to tilt the camera, which would cause the vertical lines to converge. The foreground shadow has subdued the colour of the flowers quite effectively, preventing them from being too distracting and allowing the building to be the main focus of attention.

Technical Details
6 x 4.5cm SLR camera with a 50mm shift lens, polarising and 81C warm-up filters on Fuji Velvia.

Thinking

I thought that shooting towards the light might create a more pleasing effect and walked around the garden looking for a viewpoint which would improve the lighting quality and also provide an interesting foreground.

Acting

This viewpoint seemed to fulfil both needs and from here the lighting also created a very atmospheric quality. I decided to frame the shot so that most of the cottage roof was excluded from the image as well, part of its façade – this threw more emphasis on to the the foreground and made the most of the flower colour.

Technical Details
6 x 4.5cm SLR camera with a 55–110mm zoom lens and an 81C warm-up filter on Fuji Velvia.

▲ **Technical Details**
6 x 4.5cm SLR camera with a 35mm wide-angle lens, polarising and 81EF warm-up filters on Fuji Velvia.

Rule of Thumb

Taking successful photographs of buildings often means shooting at a very specific time of day – even a slight change in the direction of sunlight can make a significant difference to the quality and effect of the image.

Technical Details
▼ 6 x 4.5cm SLR camera with a 50mm shift lens and an 81C warm-up filter on Fuji Velvia

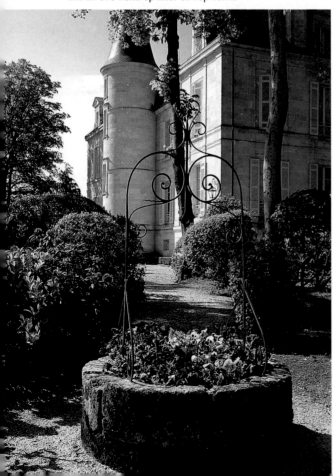

The garden of Chateau Pichon Longueville, Comtesse de Lalande in the Medoc region of France.

I'd arrived at this chateau in the very early morning to photograph its façade but could not resist stopping for a moment to shoot this ancient well, as first light was the only time this part of the garden was illuminated. I used a shift lens to eliminate some of the foreground but was unable to include all of the chateau's tower without moving further back. This would have made the well too small and I felt that by including the top of the tower I would also have too much sky in the picture.

Seeing
The sharp, clear light of this late autumn day created a very crisp, bright scene which was bordering on being too contrasty, especially on the chateau itself, where the central part of the façade was in quite deep shadow. If photographing the building had been the sole purpose of my picture I would have returned at a later time when the light was more front-on.

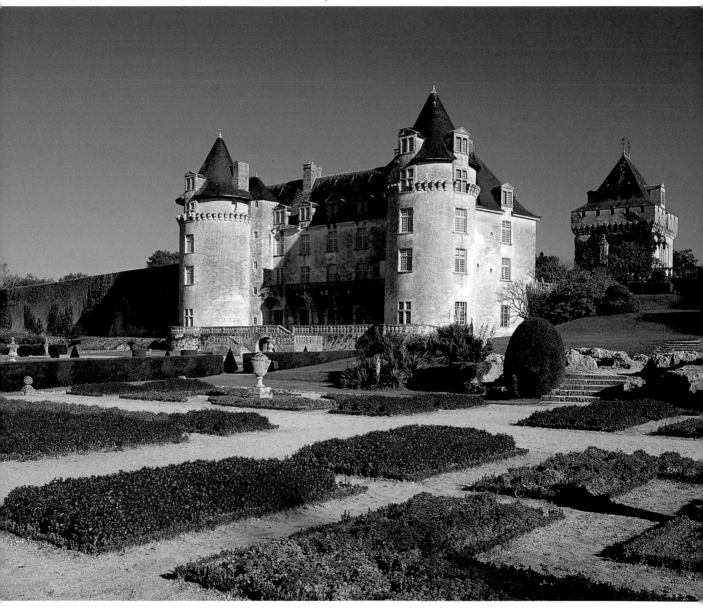

Thinking

I felt that as I wanted to show the building in the setting of its formal garden I could afford to take a much more distant viewpoint and allow the building to be quite small in the frame. I needed to take my shot quite soon as the long shadows were already beginning to encroach on the flower beds in the foreground.

Acting

I decided to use a very wide-angle lens. This allowed me to include a large area of the flower beds in the foreground, as well as the keep behind the chateau, and helped to make the shadow on the façade a bit less noticeable. I used a polarising filter to make the sky a deeper blue and an 81EF warm-up filter.

Water Features

The presence of water in a photograph invariably adds an element of interest to an image, with the opportunity to make use of its reflective nature and movement. Garden designers are equally aware of its visual potential, and many great gardens have made full use of its qualities.

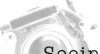

Seeing

I'd visited this famous garden on a number of occasions before but had never managed to be there when the light on this lake created an interesting enough effect. On this occasion I arrived very early, waiting for the garden to open, and the light was much more atmospheric.

Thinking

Finding a suitable viewpoint depended not only on creating the best composition, with the right lighting quality, but also on avoiding the large numbers of other visitors who had also arrived very early.

Acting

This viewpoint proved to be the best compromise. By using a very wide-angle lens I was able to include some foreground interest while shooting almost directly into the light, which created a pleasing atmospheric quality. I had to wait for a brief moment before shooting as a constant stream of people was passing along the opposite bank. I also needed to use my lens shield gadget to protect the lens from flare.

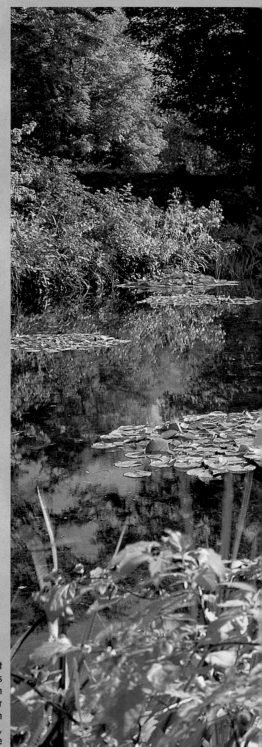

The lake at Monet's garden in Giverny near Vernon in Normandy, France

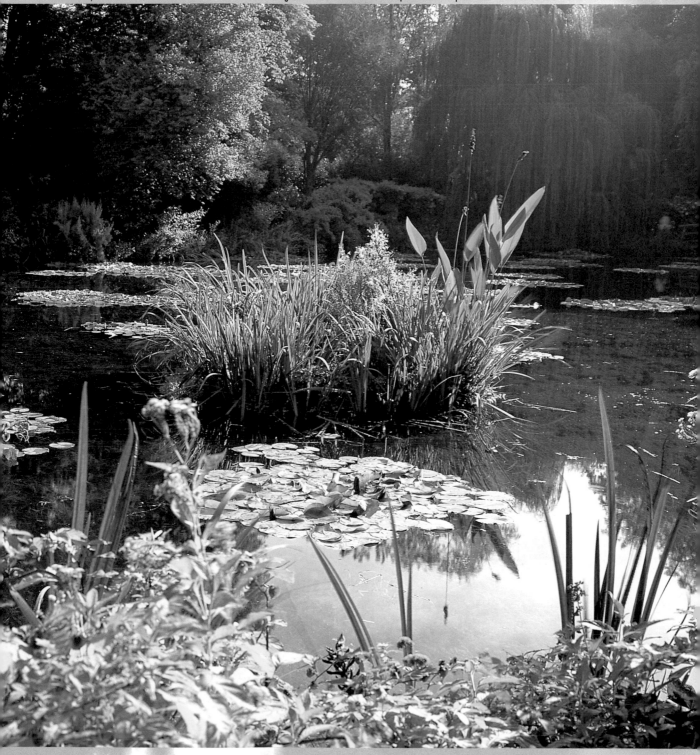

Water Features

Rule of Thumb

Photographing moving water with a slow shutter speed can create very pleasing effects, especially when it flows copiously and the shutter speed is several seconds. The effect is invariably enhanced when the water is lit softly – direct sunlight with the accompanying bright highlights tends to create a much less subtle effect.

Seeing

This popular garden is a classic example of when water is used both as a visual and an audible feature, creating a cool and peaceful ambience in a very hot place.

Thinking

I wanted to convey something of the atmosphere, but the choice of viewpoints is quite limited here and was made more so by the many visitors who thronged the relatively small space.

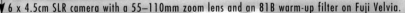

Technical Details
▼ 6 x 4.5cm SLR camera with a 55–110mm zoom lens and an 81B warm-up filter on Fuji Velvia.

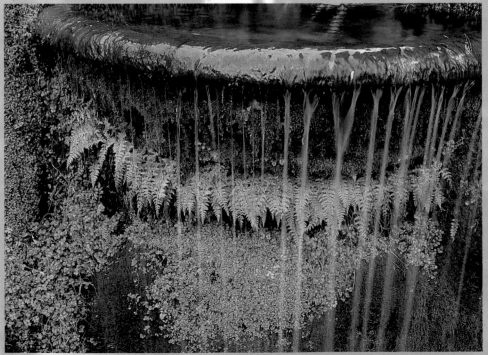

The grotto at Powerscourt Gardens near Wicklow in County Wicklow, Eire

For this shot I decided to move in close and frame the image very tightly, restricting the colour range of the image to the green of the ferns and the neutral tones of the water and stone, which has helped to accentuate the textural quality of the image. I used a slow shutter speed of about 1/2 a second which has recorded the trickle of water quite softly.

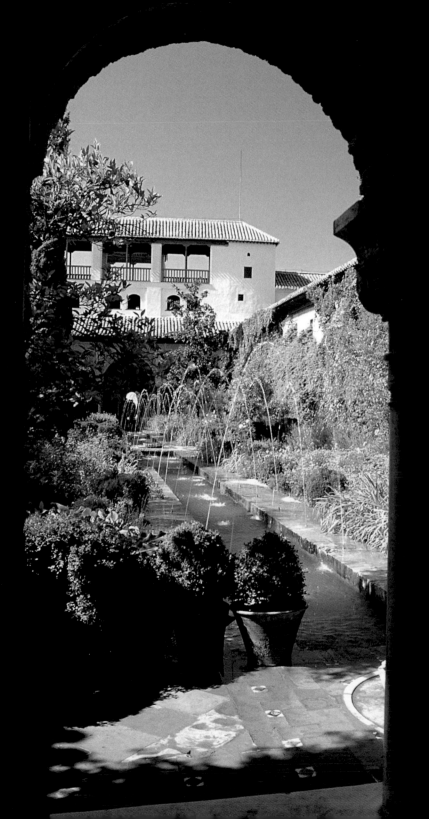

Acting

I chose a viewpoint at the **far end** of the water garden which allowed me to use the **shaded archway** as a frame to the image, creating a strong **sense of depth** and helping to enhance the peaceful and intimate nature of the place. I waited until there was a **brief gap** in the crowds before shooting.

The water garden of the Alhambra Palace in Granada, Spain

Technical Details ➤
35mm SLR camera with a 20–35mm zoom lens, polarising and 81C warm-up filters on Fuji Velvia.

Arranged Flowers

Part of the pleasure of a garden is the ability to bring flowers indoors and use them as an element of a home's decor. This is not, of course, restricted to cut flowers. The creative use of house plants, window boxes, planted containers and so on can be seen all around us, and this aspect of plant photography can be just as satisfying as photographing in a garden.

Seeing

I saw this ancient, crumbling cottage as I drove through a small village. It would have appealed to me anyway as a picture, but the flowers made it a must.

Thinking

It was an overcast day and the lighting was soft, which suited the subject very well, but I did need to crop the image quite tightly to allow the colour of the geraniums to occupy as much of the frame as possible.

Acting

I used my zoom lens to frame the image from my roadside viewpoint so that the roof line was excluded but the small shuttered window in the top-lright corner of the frame remained.

Technical Details

6 x 7cm SLR camera with a 105mm lens on Fuji Velvia.

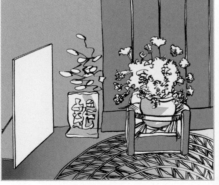

Here you can see how the reflector was placed to throw light back into the shadows and reduce the contrast of the image.

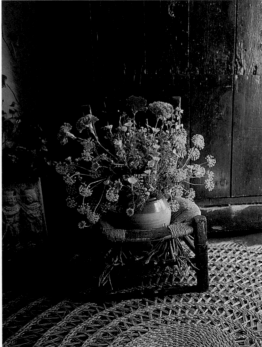

A doorway in the Andalucian village of Casares in, Spain

This delightful arrangement of flowers was what I call a 'found still life' — it just happened to be placed there in the doorway of a small restaurant. I'd been using the village street as a location while shooting photographs of some models for a travel brochure and could not resist shooting this for myself. I had with me a large white reflector which I placed on the shaded side of the arrangement to make the shadows lighter, but otherwise it was lit by natural light from the open doorway.

Rule of Thumb

Stone buildings, walls and other features invariably look more attractive if you use a warm-up filter to enhance the colour and texture of the stone.

A cottage in the Dordogne region of France

Technical Details

▼ 6 x 4.5cm SLR camera with a 55–110mm zoom an lens and an 81C warm-up filter on Fuji Velvia.

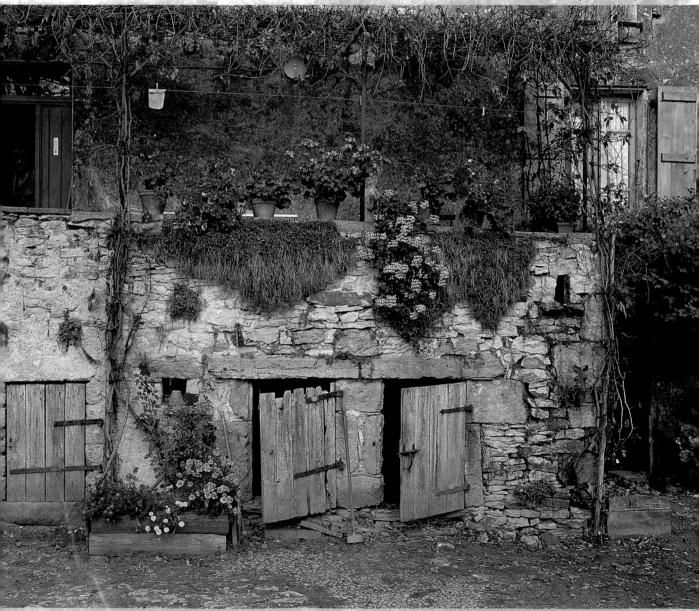

Garden Portraits

One of the most satisfying ways of photographing a garden is to treat it as a subject for a photo essay. The majority of photographs are taken with the intention of standing alone, to be viewed as single, independent images. But this can be a rather limiting way of regarding photography, and often the desire to include as much information as possible, during that single decisive moment when the exposure is made, can be a factor in producing photographs of limited visual appeal and impact. While some images are powerful enough to stand alone, hung on a gallery wall, for example, or used as a magazine cover or double-page spread, they often do not tell the viewer as much about a particular garden as a sequence of images can in the form of a photo essay.

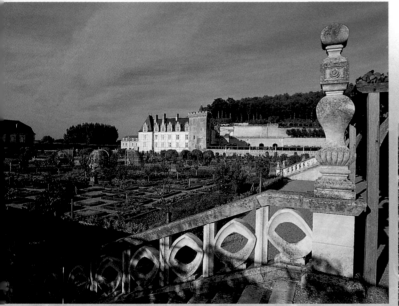

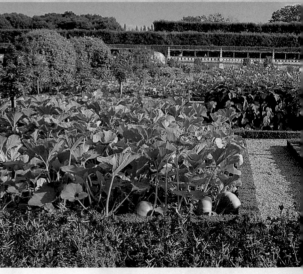

The Gardens of Chateau Villandry near Tours in the Loire Valley, France

◄ **Technical Details** ►
6 x 4.5cm SLR camera with lenses ranging from 35mm wide-angle to 210mm long-focus with polarising and warm-up filters on Fuji Velvia.

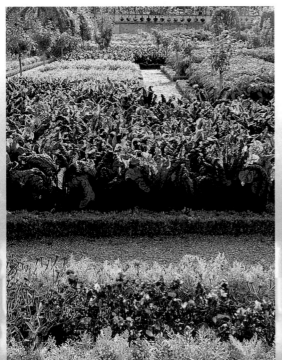

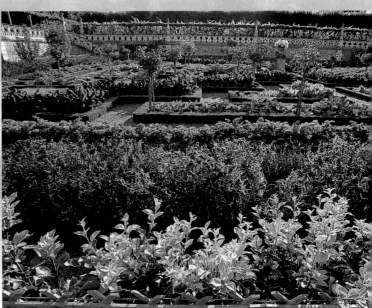

Technique

The images on the next four pages were all taken during a period of about three hours on a late-autumn afternoon with the aim of conveying an **impression** of the extent and variety of the design and planting of this unique garden together with its chateau. Shooting a garden portrait within a fairly **limited time span** helps to give the images a sense of continuity even when you have varied the viewpoints, composition, framing and lighting.

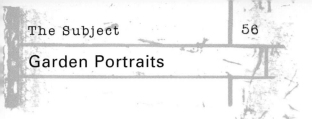

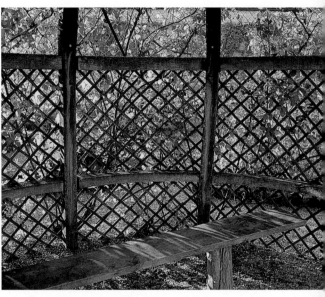

The Gardens of Chateau Villandry near Tours in the Loire Valley, France

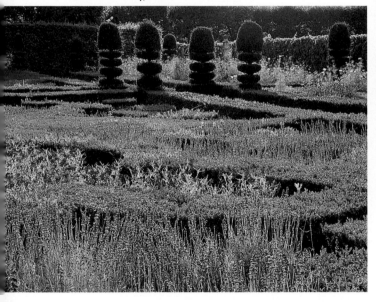

Rule of Thumb

It's always a good idea to walk around a garden several times in various directions, as it can be surprising just how differently you can see things when you approach them from a new angle and when the light is directed at them from a different position.

Technique

It can be helpful when shooting a garden portrait to think of your images in terms of a storyboard for a film or television production. For instance, you would have an establishing shot which showed something of the garden's layout and setting. You could then photograph the most important features, looking at ways of revealing strong visual qualities like colour, pattern and texture, followed perhaps by very close-up images of particular blooms or shrubs for which the garden is noted.

The key to shooting a garden portrait is the ability to think in terms of how the images you are producing will look when viewed as a collection – as they might be laid out on a double-page spread of a magazine, for instance, or as a group of framed prints on a wall.

Technical Details
6 x 4.5cm SLR camera with lenses ranging from 35mm wide-angle to 210mm long-focus with polarising and warm-up filters on Fuji Velvia.

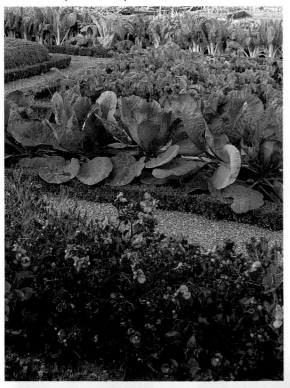

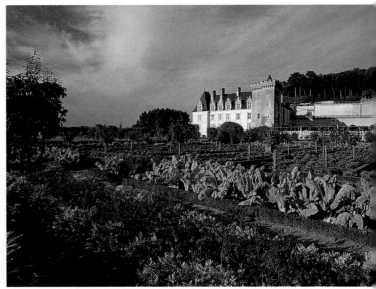

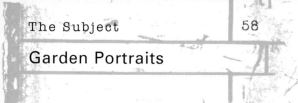

The five images on these two pages were taken during a late-summer afternoon in a much smaller and far less formal woodland garden.

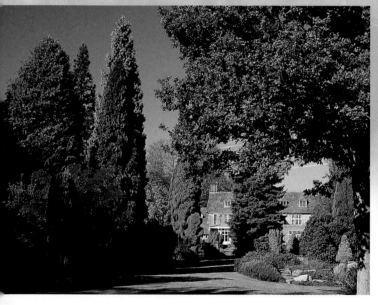

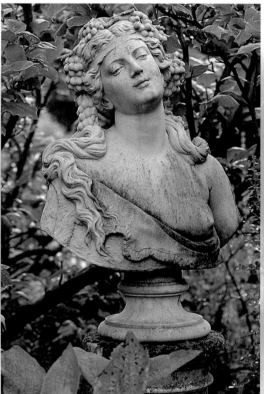

Technique

An effective way of ensuring that your pictures of a particular garden are varied enough is to make conscious changes to the way you work. If, for instance, you have been shooting with a long-focus lens, fit a wide-angle instead and, very often, a new way of seeing a place will reveal itself. In a similar way, shooting from near ground level, or from a higher viewpoint, will give a quite different perspective to a photograph taken at eye level.

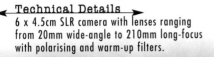

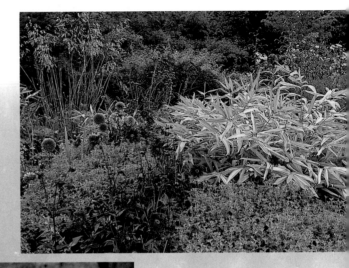

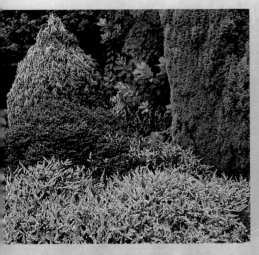

The Gardens of Great Comp near Sevenoaks in Kent, UK

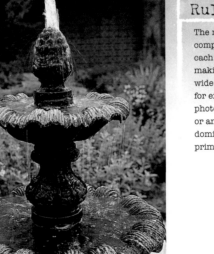

Rule of Thumb

The main thing to consider when compiling a portrait of a garden is how each picture relates to the others, making a conscious effort to alternate wide views with close-ups of plants: for example, a shot of a border with a photograph of an architectural detail, or an image where blue or green dominates, juxtaposed to one of primarily reds and yellows.

Trees & the Woodland Garden

Trees are, perhaps, the most magnificent of all
Nature's plants, not simply because of their scale
but also because of the intricacy of their construction and their ability to survive
over many centuries – trees have a history. The woodland environment also
creates a special form of plant life and this, too, offers the
photographer the opportunity to take garden photographs which are
rather different from the norm.

Seeing

I'd arrived very early on a late October morning to
photograph the chateau itself but was immediately
attracted by the large drifts of wild cyclamen
which carpeted the floor of the wood.

Thinking

The problem was to find a viewpoint which would
show enough of the plants to convey the density of the
flowers and would enable me to capture the
atmosphere of the wood itself in the beautiful
morning light.

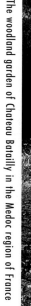

The woodland garden of Chateau Batailly in the Medoc region of France

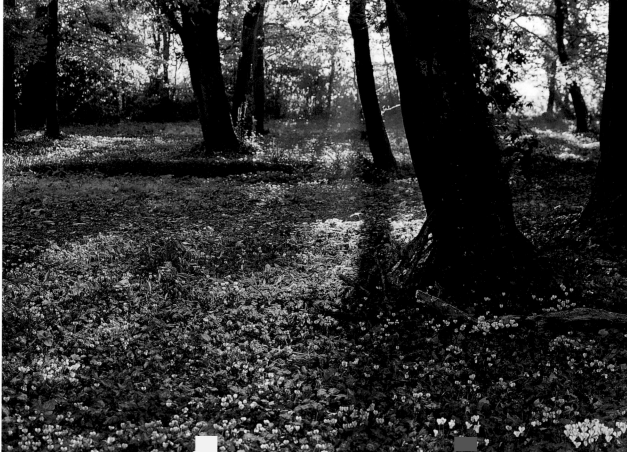

Notice how by including more of the tree the effect of its shape and the pattern of light would have been diminished.

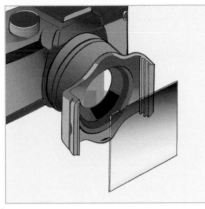

Acting

I finally settled upon this viewpoint which, with the aid of a long-focus lens, enabled me to isolate a small section of the wood where the blooms were most prolific. From here I was also able to include the shafts of sunlight filtering through the trees. This area was much brighter and needed less exposure than the foreground, so I used a neutral-graduated filter to help balance the two areas. I set a small aperture to obtain maximum depth of field.

Technique

To take a series of photographs of a specific tree at intervals through the course of a year can be a very satisfying and fascinating way of building a collection of photographs.

Technical Details →
35mm SLR camera with a 20–35mm zoom lens, polarising and 81C warm-up filters on Fuji Velvia.

← **Technical Details**
6 x 4.5cm SLR camera with a 105–210mm zoom lens and a neutral-graduated filter on Fuji Velvia.

The garden of Hever Castle near Edenbridge in Kent, UK

I saw this elegant oak tree in the woodland garden of Hever Castle in the early summer. The foliage had not yet reached its full density and I was attracted by the dappled sunlight which had filtered through the leaves on to its trunk and branches, creating a very pleasing pattern. I framed the image quite tightly to emphasise this area and used a polarising filter to increase the colour saturation of the leaves and sky together with an 81C warm-up filter.

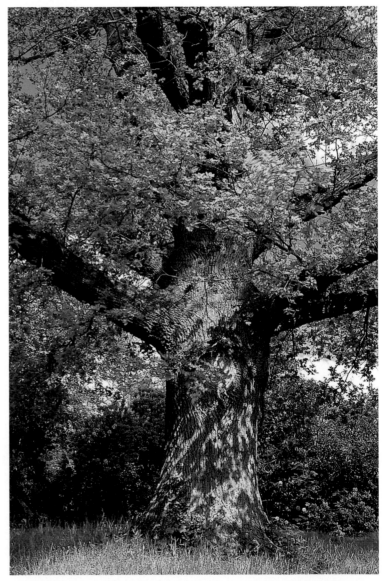

Ornaments & Details

From statues, wooden benches, archways and plant pots to fountains, walls and gazebos, ornaments are an important aspect of garden design and can contribute greatly to the interest and composition of photographs, either as the main feature of an image or in conjunction with wider views of a garden.

Seeing

This shot was taken in the winter when there was a distinct lack of colour and foliage and I was looking for other aspects of the garden to help provide interesting subjects when this rather bizarre satyr caught my eye.

Thinking

I liked the rather stark skeletons of the pollarded trees. I found the lighting on them particularly pleasing, and I decided that it could be effective to combine them with the satyr in some way.

Acting

I found a viewpoint which enabled me to place the statue between two of the trees, as well as allowing me to include part of the topiary, while the more distant chateau's outbuilding provided an additional element of interest to the composition. I used my zoom lens on a longish setting to frame the image quite tightly with 81C warm-up and polarising filters to increase the density of the blue sky.

Technical Details

▼ 6 x 4.5cm SLR camera with a 105–210mm zoom lens, polarising and 81C warm-up filters on Fuji Velvia.

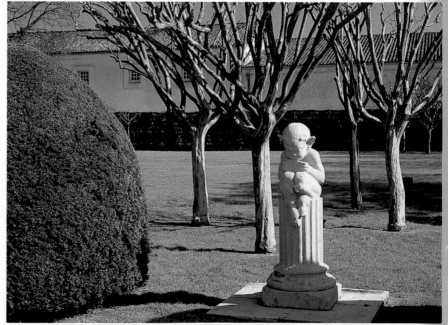

The garden of Chateau Mouton Rothschild in the Medoc region of France

The gardens of Hever Castle near Edenbridge in Kent, UK

I included the stone bench and plaque in this shot of an autumnal boston ivy as these neutral tones accentuated the vivid colour of the foliage. I chose a frontal viewpoint in order to eliminate the impression of perspective and give the image a more graphic quality.

Technical Details

35mm SLR camera with a 35–70mm zoom lens and an 81B warm-up filter on Fuji Velvia.

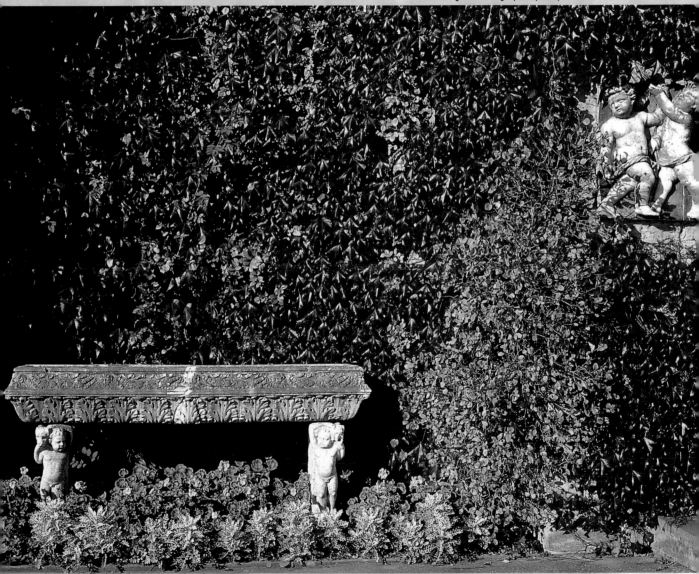

Ornaments & Details

Rule of Thumb

You can often help to make a subject stand out well from the background when there is some distance between them by the use of differential focusing. Simply focus on the main subject and select a wide aperture to limit the depth of field. The effect will be greater when a long-focus lens is used.

Seeing

This scarecrow, attending a scarecrow festival, adds a real touch of humour to this garden and provided Julien Busselle with a great subject for this picture.

Thinking

Julien felt that the phoney crow needed to be emphasised as it could have easily become a little lost in the composition and he also wanted to carry the smile, which the scarecrow invariably provokes, over to his picture.

Acting

Choosing a low viewpoint has enabled most of the scarecrow to be silhouetted against the sky which has emphasised its raggedy shape and at the same time given the crow considerable prominence. Julien framed the shot so that the crow was placed on the spot where lines dividing the image into thirds would meet – the strongest place in the frame – and then tilted the camera sideways slightly to give the scarecrow a rather jaunty air.

Rule of Thumb

When photographing ornaments and details it's important to ensure that they stand out well from the background. Choosing a viewpoint from where there is a strong tonal or colour contrast between the subject and the immediate background area is one of the most effective ways.

Technical Details
▼ 35mm SLR camera with a 35–70mm zoom lens on Fuji Velvia.

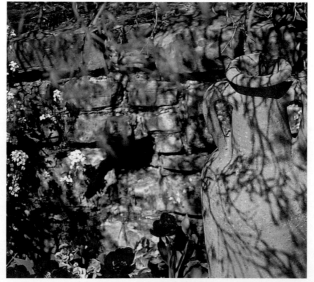

In this picture by Julien Busselle, the sunlight has created a very pleasing pattern on the ceramic urn, without which it would have been rather bland. Julien chose a viewpoint which created a degree of perspective on the wall behind using a widish aperture so that the background details were slightly unsharp, thereby giving more emphasis to the urn.

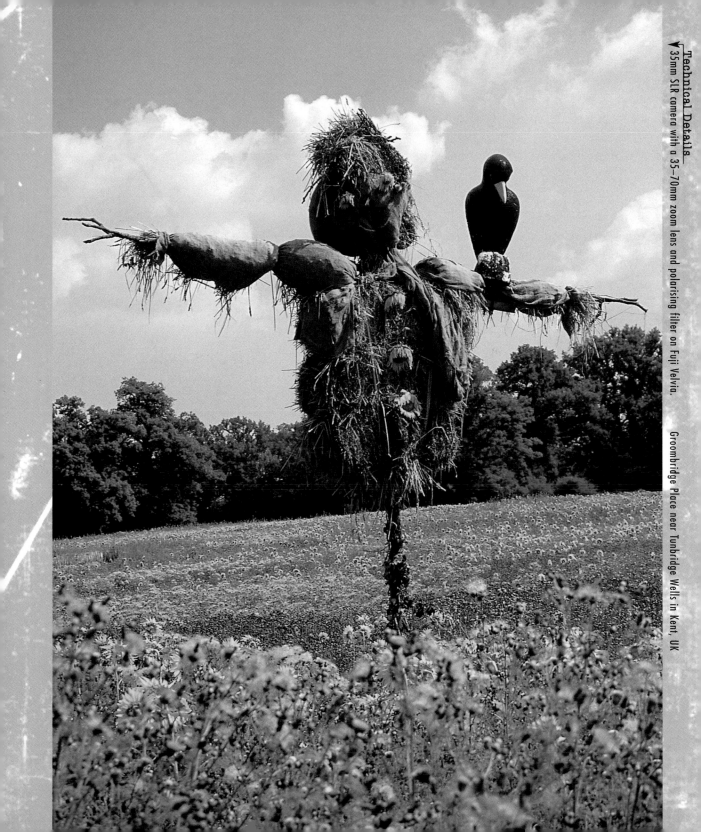

Technical Details
▼ 35mm SLR camera with a 35–70mm zoom lens and polarising filter on Fuji Velvia.   Groombridge Place near Tunbridge Wells in Kent, UK

The Vegetable Garden

Flowers and shrubs are by no means the only subjects of photographic interest in a garden – fruit and vegetables can also provide a wealth of visual possibilities. They invariably have very pleasing shapes, colours and textures which can be used to create quite striking images, either when photographed *in situ* or as arranged still lifes or close-ups.

Seeing

This still-life photograph was taken to illustrate a brochure to suggest the use of home-grown food. In fact, the vegetables all came from a local supermarket and the wooden trug was borrowed from a garden centre.

Thinking

Needing to find a suitable background for the set-up, I visited a local allotment and found this immaculate vegetable garden, the owner of which was happy to let me set up my shot in front of his impressive bean row.

Acting

I used a small wooden table as a means of placing the arrangement at a suitable height and chose a position so the sunlight was at the most effective angle. The shadows it cast were, however, rather too dense, so I placed a large white reflector on the shadowed side of the set-up to throw some light back into them and reduce the contrast of the image. I used a small aperture as I wanted the bean row in the background to be as sharp as possible.

Tapeley Park, Instow in North Devon, UK

This shot of apples on a tree by Julien Busselle has a quite powerful effect, largely because of the very limited colour range and the colour density and saturation. Shooting almost directly upwards, Julien has placed the very green apples and foliage against a deep blue sky which he's accentuated further by the use of a polarising filter.

Technical Details ➤
6 x 4.5cm SLR camera with a 105–210mm zoom lens and a polarising filter on Fuji Velvia.

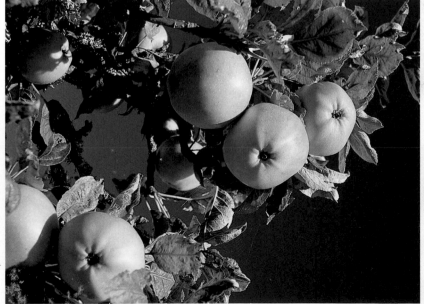

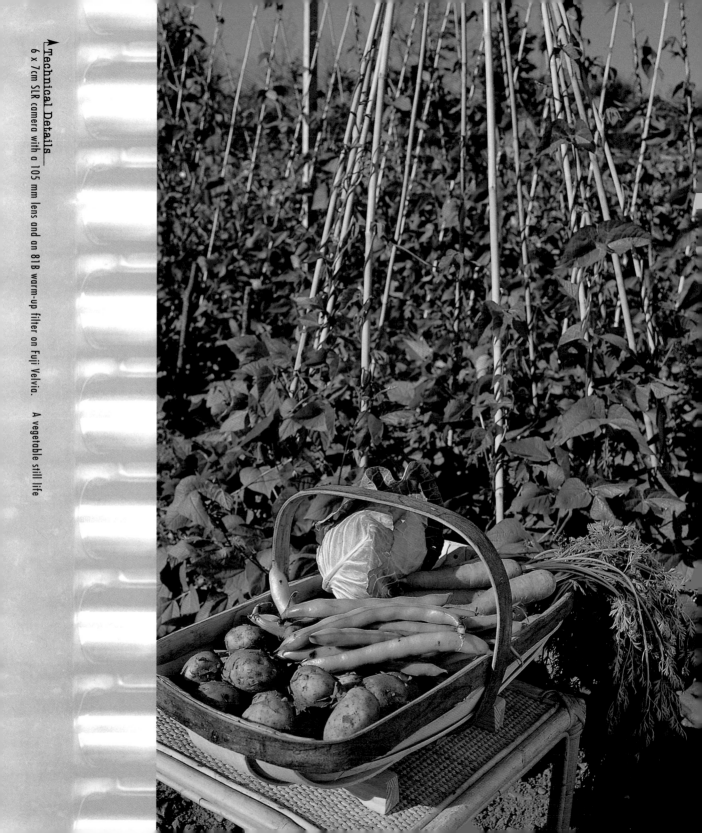

▲ **Technical Details**
6 x 7cm SLR camera with a 105 mm lens and an 81B warm-up filter on Fuji Velvia.   A vegetable still life

The Art of Composition for
Landscape Photography

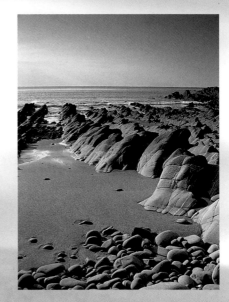

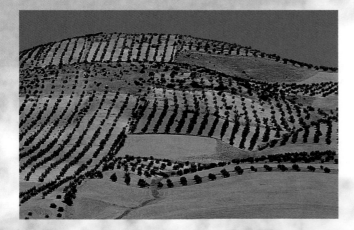

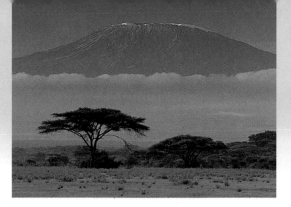

2

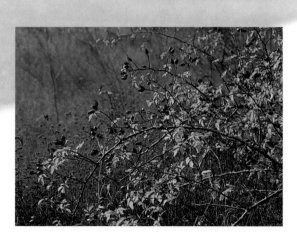

The art of composition involves organising the elements of a scene within the camera's viewfinder in the most telling way. With subjects like still lives and portraits the subject itself can be organised but with landscape photography the composition can only be altered by the choice of viewpoint and the way in which the image is framed.

The Importance of Viewpoint

The ability to select a particular aspect of a scene, and to arrange it in the most pleasing way, is largely dependent upon the choice of viewpoint, and this is one of the most important decisions a photographer can make before taking a photograph. Many inexperienced photographers will shoot their pictures from the place where they were first aware of a potential picture but, when time allows, it pays to explore all the possibilities before making your exposure.

Seeing

This is one of the most photogenic sections of the Tarn Gorges which are quite difficult to photograph in a way which suggest the sheer spectacle of the river. At this point a platform has been provided for tourists to enjoy the view and the raised viewpoint does help to create a much more dramatic perspective of the gorge than is possible from the river bank.

Acting

I can claim very little credit for the sheer luck of finding this very atmospheric lighting on this visit to the river, and I have visited the same spot several times since and never found anything like as interesting. I needed to use a wide-angle lens to frame the image in the way I wanted and used an 81C warm-up filter to offset a potential blue cast. I also used a polarising filter to increase the colour saturation and to subdue the highlights on the water, as well as a neutral-graduated filter to prevent the bright sky from overexposing.

Thinking

The risk with using viewpoints like these is that you finish up with the same, often rather bland, snapshot which everyone else who visits the site has taken.

The Gorges of the River Tarn near Millau in the Midi Pyrenees region of France

Near Merida in the Extramaduran region of Spain

This photograph was taken on a very grey, overcast day but my attention was caught by the mass of white and purple wild flowers below the oak trees. I chose a viewpoint which placed the most concentrated area of colour in front of a group of trees where no daylight was visible between them, as this would have diluted the effect of the colour. I framed the shot tightly using a long-focus lens to exclude unwanted details, especially the sky which was white and featureless.

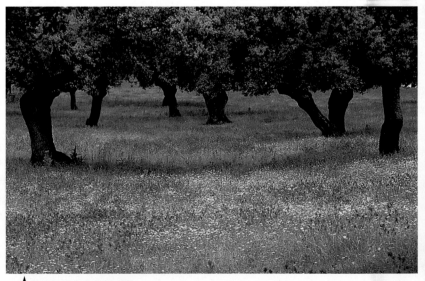

Technical Details
35mm SLR camera with a 75–300mm zoom lens and an 81B warm-up filter on Fuji Velvia.

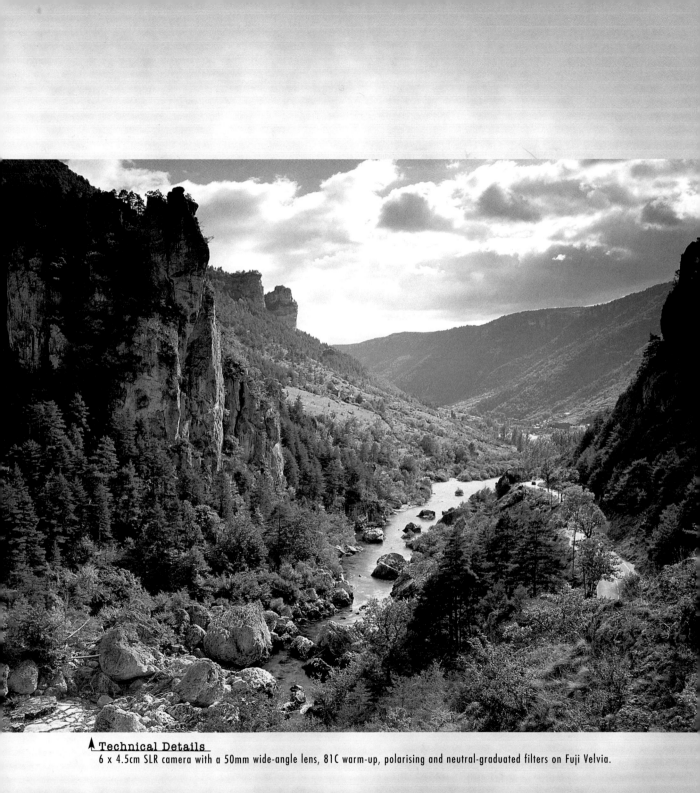

▲ Technical Details
6 x 4.5cm SLR camera with a 50mm wide-angle lens, 81C warm-up, polarising and neutral-graduated filters on Fuji Velvia.

Rule of Thumb

When looking for a viewpoint it's worth
looking behind you as well as towards
your subject as, in this way, you will
sometimes find objects which can be
used effectively as foreground interest.

Seeing

I'd driven up this mountain road looking for a place
which would give me a good view of the mountain
range on the other side of the valley and thought that
somewhere at this height would be fine.

Thinking

It was a sunny but hazy day and the lighting was
less than crisp. Consequently, although the snow-
covered mountain-top was well-defined against the
sky, the green slopes below were rather flatly lit
and lacked any real bite.

Acting

I looked around for some possible foreground interest which might add an
element of colour or contrast and found this clump of grasses and yellow flowers. I had
to use a very close viewpoint as I wanted to see over the foreground into the
valley below to heighten the feeling of depth and distance. I used a wide-angle lens to
include enough of the foreground and the sky and set a small aperture to
ensure adequate depth of field.

The Esterel Massif near St Raphael in the Var region of France

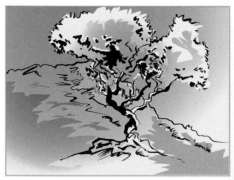

See how a more distant viewpoint would have caused
the tree to the mask the crucial area of the mountain.

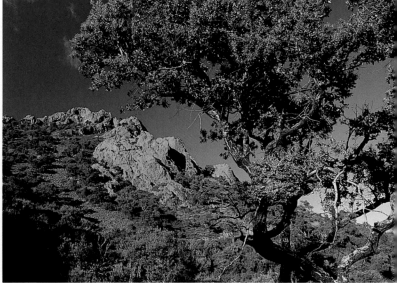

The red rocks are the most striking feature of this
mountain range and on this occasion the late afternoon
light was creating quite bold relief and enhancing their
colour. I thought that the twisted pine tree would
provide both an interesting foreground and a useful
element of contrast for the rocks and blue sky but I
found that to use the tree as a frame and to see the
top of the mountain I had to use a very close, low
viewpoint which required the use of a wide-angle lens
in order to include enough of the scene.

Technical Details
35mm SLR camera with a 20–35mm zoom lens,
81C warm-up and polarising filters on Fuji Velvia.

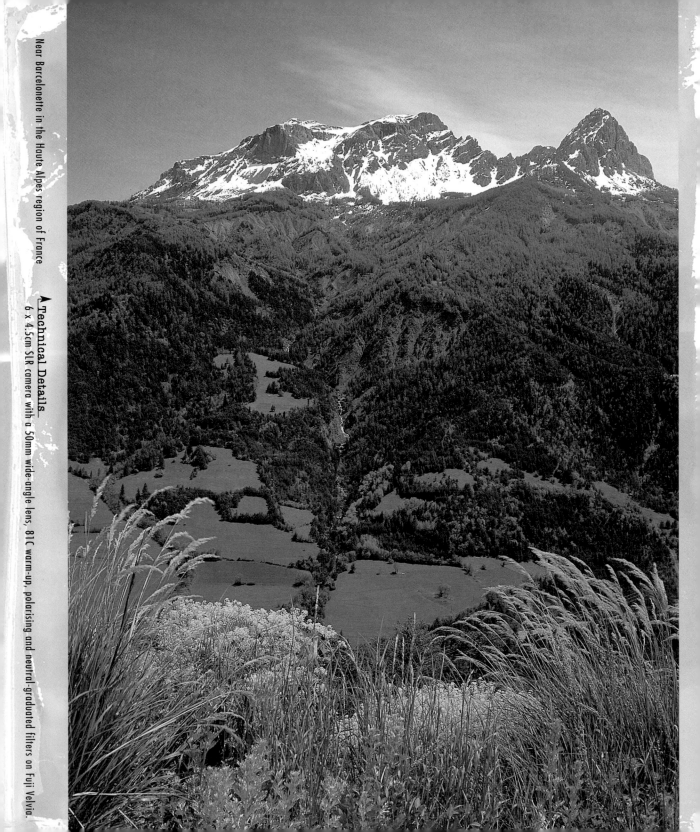

Near Barcelonette in the Haute Alpes region of France

▲ Technical Details
6 x 4.5cm SLR camera with a 50mm wide-angle lens, 81C warm-up, polarising and neutral-graduated filters on Fuji Velvia.

Framing the Image

The camera's viewfinder should be considered as the equivalent of a painter's blank canvas. While a photographer has far less control over the details included in the viewfinder it is, nevertheless, his choice and only by making the best choices are the most telling images created. Be aware of any details which are distracting or unpleasing to the eye and if they cannot be eliminated or minimised acceptably by the choice of viewpoint and the way the image is framed, the best solution may well be not to take the picture as it will almost certainly disappoint.

Seeing

For these two photographs Julien Busselle explored a number of ways of framing the image. In the first instance it was the almost unreal quality which the sunlight created on the sculpted rocks which appealed to him and he decided to frame the image so that just this group of rocks were featured in the photograph.

Thinking

Julien became more aware of the possibilities of including closer foreground details in the image and also allowing the distant sea and horizon to come into the top of the frame.

Acting

He moved to a more distant viewpoint, changed the horizontal format to an upright and then widened the setting on his zoom lens to include the additional details he wanted. He used a polarising filter to increase the colour saturation of the sand and to control the bright highlights on the sea and an 81B warm-up filter to eliminate the possibility of a blue cast.

Technique

Many inexperienced photographers use a camera's viewfinder like a gun sight, concentrating on the centre of the image and being only vaguely aware of the other details which are included. This often results in the inclusion of unwanted details and a centrally placed focus of interest, which is seldom the best position. It's best to look inwardly from the edges of the frame, so you become more aware of how all the elements of the image relate to each other.

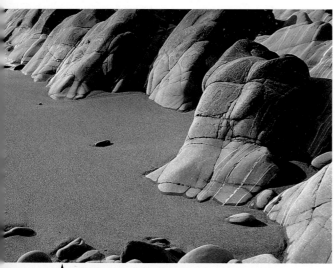

Technical Details

6 x 4.5cm SLR camera with a 55–110mm zoom lens, 81C warm-up and polarising filters on Fuji Velvia.

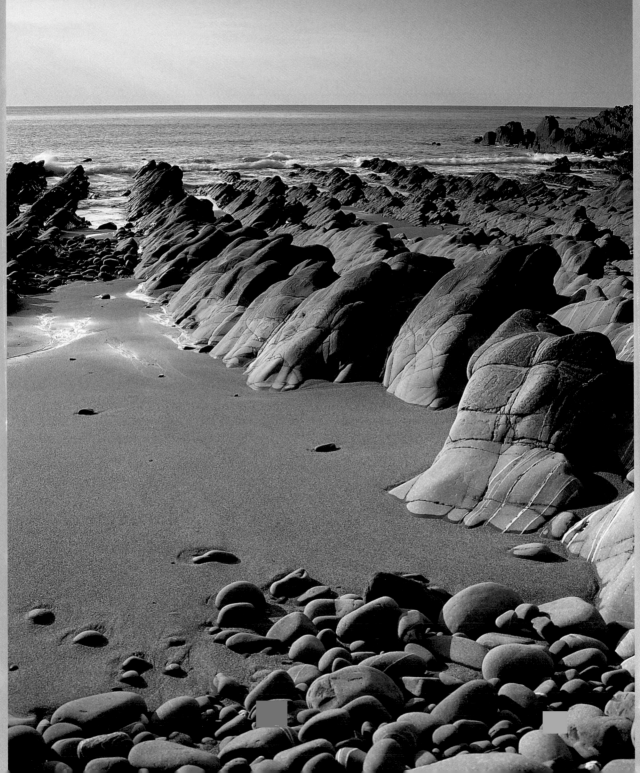

Using Shapes & Patterns

All photographs depend for their effect on a number of individual visual elements, and the most successful photographs are usually those in which one or more of these elements is boldly and clearly defined. The outline or shape of a subject is the element which usually first identifies it, and a photograph with a dominant shape invariably has a strong initial impact. The shape may not necessarily be that of a specific object — it could be simply that which is defined by an area of highlight, shadow or colour. A shape can also be one which is created by the juxtaposition of objects within a scene, such as a line of trees or a cloud formation.

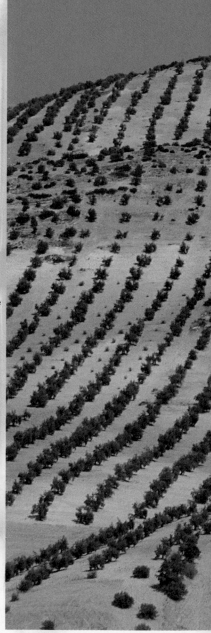

Near Jaen in Andalucia, Spain

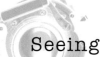

Seeing

I was driving down this small valley late on a spring afternoon as the sun was just beginning to set below the top of the steep hill on the opposite side of the valley. I suddenly saw this scene where the two trees almost appeared to be artificially lit.

Thinking

I chose a viewpoint from where the trees were close together but clearly separated and framed the image tightly to exclude the bright sky above the opposite hillside and to give full emphasis to the trees.

Acting

As the sun was shining directly on to my lens and causing flare I needed to use my lens-shield gadget to overcome this. I also used a neutral-graduated filter to ensure the shadow behind the tops of the trees was as dark as possible.

Near Aubenas in the Ardèche region of France

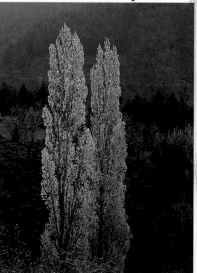

Technical Details ➤

6 x 4.5cm SLR camera with a 105–210mm zoom lens, 81C warm-up and neutral-graduated filters on Fuji Velvia.

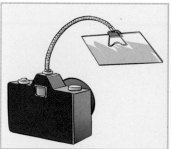

This is my lens-shield gadget attached to the camera's accessory shoe.

Technical Details
35mm SLR camera with a 75–300mm zoom lens, 81C warm-up and polarising filters on Fuji Velvia.

It was the near-sepia quality of the sun-bleached Andalucian hillside which appealed to me in this image, combined with the way the pattern of olive trees seemed to echo the curving shape of the hill. I used a long-focus lens to isolate the most effective part of the scene with an 81C warm-up filter to accentuate the warm colour of the soil and a polariser to increase the colour saturation of the rather hazy sky.

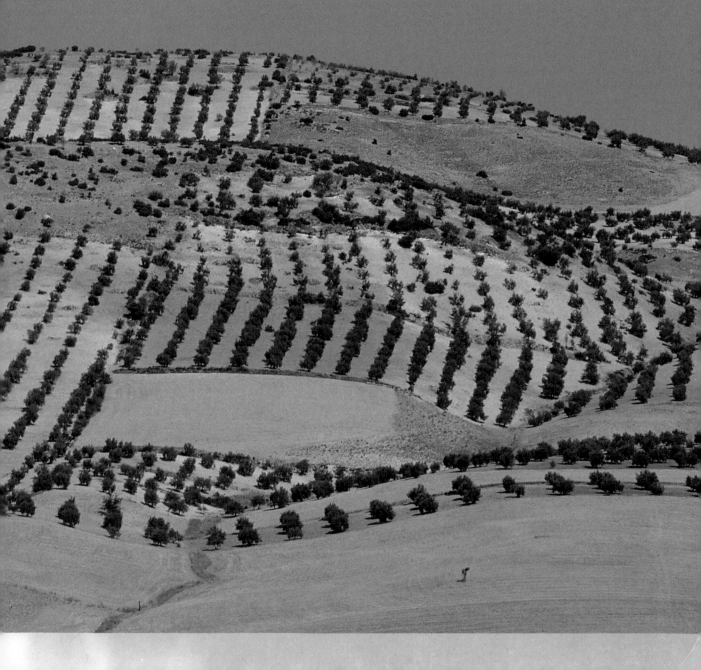

Seeing

This huge mountain is a stunning sight and visible from many places in this part of Kenya. Much of the time, however, its snow-capped peak is shrouded in cloud during the day and one of the best chances of seeing it is in the early morning. I was staying in a camp near this viewpoint and had seen this nicely shaped isolated tree during the previous day, thinking that it would provide strong additional interest for a shot of the mountain and would create an effective contrast to the smooth shape of Kilimanjaro.

Thinking

I got up long before dawn on the next day and drove to the spot, delighted to discover that the peak was clear of cloud and that the mist at ground-level made the tree stand out in strong relief.

Acting

I chose a viewpoint which balanced the tree comfortably with the bulk of the mountain and used a long-focus lens from some distance away to make sure the tree did not seem too large in proportion to it. Then I waited until the rising sun just caught the mountain top and used both polarising and neutral-graduated filters to add some strength to the quite subtle tones.

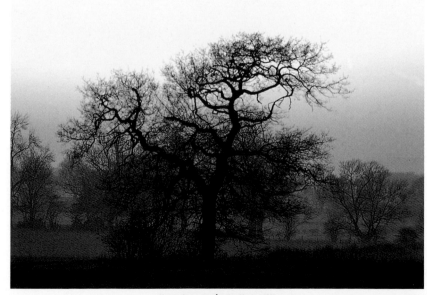

Near Sevenoaks in Kent, UK

<u>Technical Details</u>
35mm SLR camera with an 80–200mm zoom lens, neutral-graduated and polarising filters on Fuji Velvia.

Mount Kilimanjaro seen from Amboseli, Kenya

<u>Technical Details</u>
35mm SLR camera with a 150–500mm zoom lens on Fuji Velvia

I went out one winter's evening to try out a new long-focus lens and saw this distant tree just after the sun had set. I particularly liked the quality which the shapes and patterns of the bare branches had when silhouetted against the bright orangy pink sky. I used my camera's mirror lock and delayed action setting to avoid the risk of camera shake.

Using Perspective

Perspective is the effect created by the diminishing size of objects as they recede from the camera, as you can see when looking down a tree-lined avenue, for instance, or when a small rock in the close foreground appears to be as large as a distant mountain. It is this effect which helps to give an image a sense of depth and distance and also contributes to the impression of solidity and the three-dimensional quality which a photograph can have. An image which has little sense of perspective tends to have a more graphic and painterly quality.

Rule of Thumb

The effect of perspective varies according to the relative distances between the camera, the nearest objects and those furthest away. If the image includes both foreground objects and distant ones the perspective effect will be accentuated. But if there is no immediate foreground and all the principle objects are some distance away from the camera there will be a minimal suggestion of perspective and objects will be shown close to their true relative size.

Seeing

It was a perfect summer's day, with a dense blue sky and sharp clear sunlight when I visited this location, one of my favourites. If anything, the lighting was almost too contrasty for some situations but I felt that the quite stark quality would work well with this shot of a chalky track.

Thinking

The two elements which appealed to me were the effect of the track leading away from the camera and the small group of very bright white clouds just above the horizon. Although I think the shot would have worked without it, the small tree near the cloud was a bonus.

Acting

I chose a viewpoint which placed the most dominant cloud more or less on the intersection of thirds and framed the shot using a wide-angle lens, tilting the camera down to include as much of the track in the foreground as possible in order to exaggerate the perspective. I used a polarising filter to make the contrast between cloud and sky as strong as possible and an 81C warm-up filter to offset a potential blue cast.

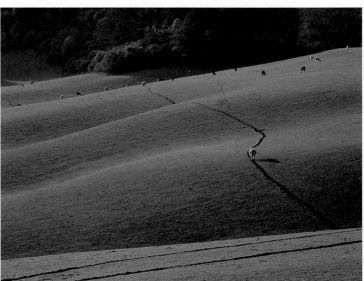

The North Downs near Wrotham in Kent

I saw this picture just before sunset on a summer's evening and was struck by the lovely contoured quality the low sun had created on the rolling downs. I used a long-focus lens to home in on the most well-defined area of the scene which at the same time has given the impression of compressed perspective and framed the image so that the track and lone cow were in the strongest position.

Technical Details
6 x 4.5cm SLR camera with a 300mm lens on Fuji Velvia.

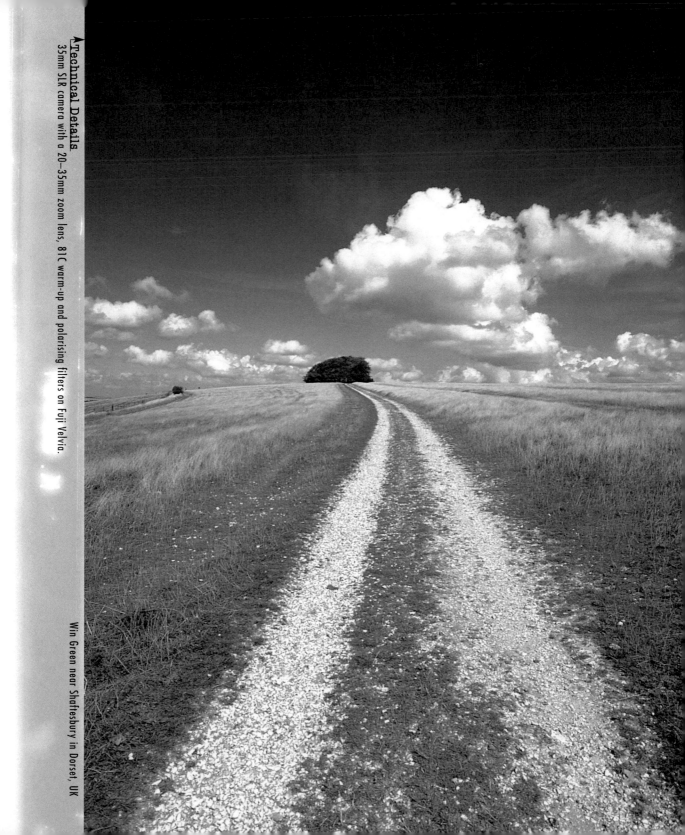

Technical Details

35mm SLR camera with a 20–35mm zoom lens, 81C warm-up and polarising filters on Fuji Velvia.

Win Green near Shaftesbury in Dorset, UK

▲Technical Details
35mm SLR camera with a 20–35mm zoom lens, polarising and 81EF warm-up filters on Fuji Velvia.

Seeing

In landscape photography, anything which creates a contrast with the dominant colours of blue and green tends to have a striking effect and this rape field caught my eye. The pair of silhouetted trees on the horizon were also a valuable element as were the strong blue sky and white clouds.

Thinking

I still felt the image needed something else to create a really bold image and I thought that including this small section of the rustic wooden fence in the foreground would add interest and heighten the sense of depth and distance.

Rule of Thumb

Because wide-angle lenses enable you to include both very close and far distant details in the same image they have the effect of exaggerating the perspective effect. A long-focus lens, on the other hand, will enable you to eliminate close foreground details and will, accordingly, lessen the impression of perspective.

Technical Details
▼ 35mm SLR camera with a 300mm lens on Fuji Velvia.

A spring meadow near Valdepenas in La Mancha, Spain

I spotted this blaze of colour from some distance away but, as is often the case, when I approached the patch of flowers more closely the effect was less dramatic. I decided to use a more distant viewpoint and a long-focus lens to isolate the most striking area of the field and compress the colour effect within the frame. Even if I used a small aperture the depth of field would be limited so I focused on what I felt was the most dominant plane and allowed the other details to be out of focus.

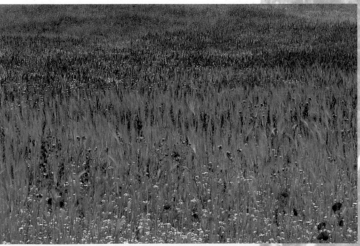

Acting

I used my **wide-angle** zoom at its widest setting so the fence almost filled the bottom third of the frame and the sky the top third. I used a **polarising filter** to increase the colour saturation and the relief between clouds and sky and an 81EF **warm-up filter** to offset a potential blue cast.

The Darent Valley near Otford in Kent, UK

The sky can be a very important element in landscape photography and the position the horizon occupies is likely to be a dominant force in the composition of an image. The standard advice is to place it along a line which divides the image into thirds and as a general rule it should not divide the picture into two equal halves. But a great deal depends upon the nature of the sky and also on details or objects which extend from the landscape into the sky. Ultimately, it is a question of placing the horizon in a way which creates a pleasing balance between all of these elements.

Seeing

I saw this lone tree as I drove along a small country road and it seemed like a potentially **strong image**. It was not until I got out of my car that I saw the solitary cloud above it.

Thinking

I could see that the cloud was both moving and evaporating and realised I only had a **short time** to take my shot. I set up very quickly and chose a viewpoint which placed the cloud more or less directly above the tree.

Technical Details
6 x 4.5cm SLR camera with a 55–110mm zoom lens, 81B warm-up and polarising filters on Fuji Velvia.

Rule of Thumb

The sky is invariably proportionately brighter than the landscape below it, because it is, in effect, a part of the light source. When a significant area of bright sky is included in the viewfinder it can cause a degree of underexposure and it is best to take your reading with the camera tilted downwards to exclude the sky.

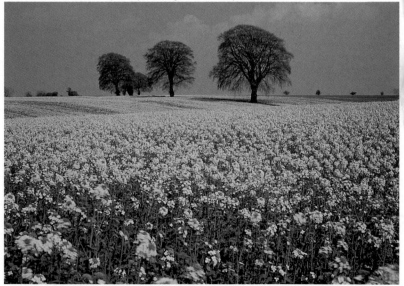

A rape field in spring near Cheltenham in Gloucestershire, UK

I was attracted to the group of trees, just coming into leaf, on the horizon of this shot. I chose a viewpoint which created the best separation between them and used a wide-angle lens to include a large amount of foreground and to emphasise the effect of perspective. I framed the shot so that only a small section of the rather weak sky was included.

Acting

I framed the image to place the tree slightly off centre and to exclude a fence along the bottom edge of the field and include a small area of sky above the cloud. I used a polarising filter to increase the colour saturation and relief between sky and cloud, and added an 81C warm-up filter to eliminate the risk of a blue cast.

▲ Technical Details
35mm SLR camera with a 35–70mm zoom lens, 81C warm-up and polarising filters on Fuji Velvia.

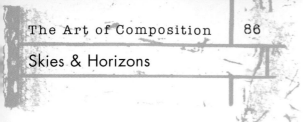

The banks of the River Gironde near Pauillac in the Medoc region of France

The sky alone was the sole reason for taking this shot. I looked very hard for a suitable foreground to add interest and more strength to the composition but without success. I decided it was worth it anyway and framed the image in a way which allowed the sky to occupy most of the frame and which also placed the small gap in the trees on the distant bank and the reflections in the water in the strongest position as a focus of interest.

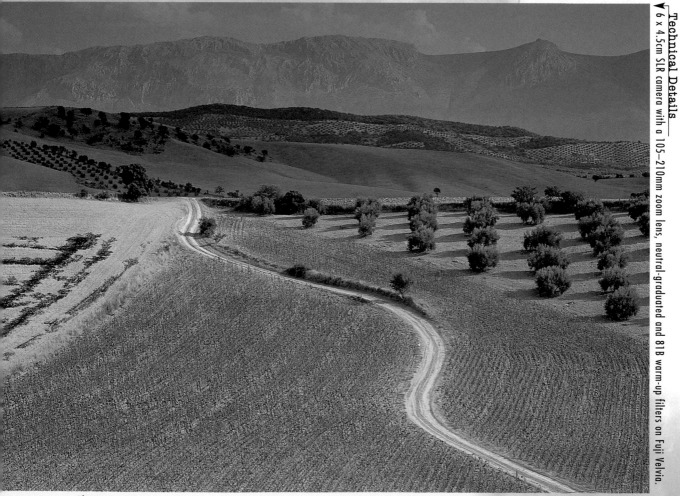

Technical Details
6 x 4.5cm SLR camera with a 105–210mm zoom lens, neutral-graduated and 81B warm-up filters on Fuji Velvia.

The Sierra Magina near Jaen in Andalucia, Spain

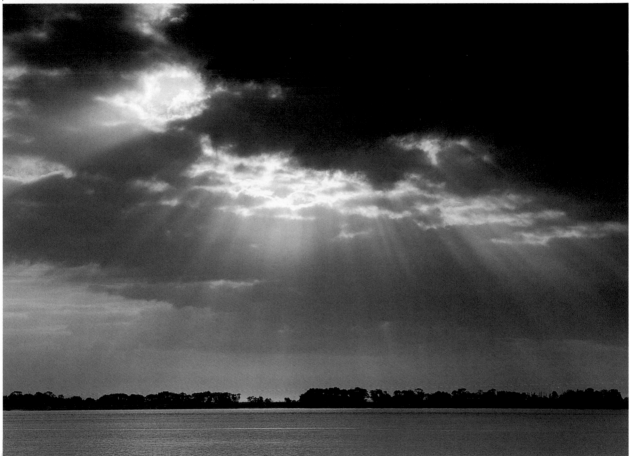

Seeing

It was a late autumn afternoon when I saw this scene while travelling through the northern part of Andalucia where the parched landscape has this almost sepia quality. It was this which appealed to me along with the striking textural effect created by the low angle of the sun.

Thinking

The negative factor was the presence of a rather weak, hazy sky but this was offset to a degree by the fact that the mountain below was in shadow which helped to create sufficient contrast.

Acting

I decided to frame the shot so that only a small area of the sky was included in the image and used a neutral-graduated filter to make both the sky and shadowed mountain as dark as possible.

Technique

If the sky does not make a positive contribution to the image, and there is nothing of importance which rises above it, it is best to consider cropping it out altogether or to include only a very small strip to define the horizon.

Landscape in Close-up

Moving much closer to objects within the landscape can often reveal details of astonishing beauty. Close-up photography can make a textured surface seem as big and important as a distant landscape and it's possible to reveal shapes and patterns in many natural forms, like trees and rocks, which would otherwise pass unnoticed. Taking a much closer view of the landscape can heighten your sense of perception and help you to see new ways of approaching a subject and of composing images.

Seeing

I was initially drawn by the pattern which the lichen created on the rock and the striking contrast it created with the darker tone and texture of the stone and considered using a very close viewpoint to make this the sole feature of the image.

Thinking

When I set up my camera and tripod I became aware of the more striking contrast between the dark greenish colour of the rock and the rust-brown hue of the dead leaves.

Acting

When I looked through the viewfinder and experimented with the viewpoint and framing I found that by cropping the rock in this way and including an equal area of leaves at the side and base of the image it created a quite bold, graphic shape and the colours seemed to enhance each other. I used an extension tube to allow the lens to focus at a close distance.

The Forest of Fontainebleu in the region of Ile de France, France

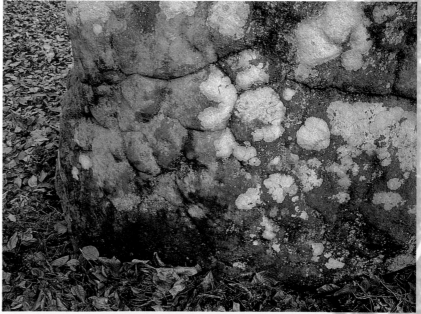

Technical Details
6 x 4.5cm SLR camera with a 55–110mm zoom lens and an extension tube on Fuji Velvia.

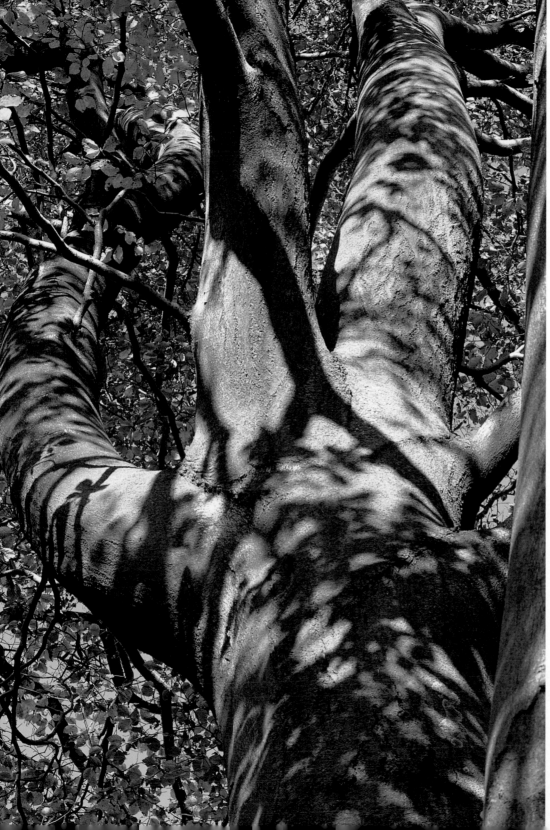

Technical Details
35mm SLR camera with a 35—70mm zoom lens and 81B warm-up filter on Fuji Velvia.

Knole Park near Sevenoaks in Kent, UK

The combination of the shape created by the trunk and twisting branches of this fine old beech tree and the shadows the sunlight had created as it filtered through the foliage made this image work for me. In order to see this clearly I had to use a very close viewpoint, from almost against the tree trunk, and I framed the shot so that the strongest combination of shape and shadow was included in the image.

Rule of Thumb

Depth of field becomes increasingly limited as the lens is focused at closer distances and it is necessary to use a small aperture for subjects where you want to have the images sharp overall, especially if they are not flat on to the camera.

Seeing

This shot was taken in winter on an overcast day when the light was not creating enough contrast for long-distance landscapes. But this waterfall caught my eye, partly because of its intriguing shape as the water coursed down over the rocks and partly because of the pattern and texture created by the bare branches of the neighbouring trees which were heightened by the monochromatic quality of the scene.

Thinking

I needed to make the waterfall quite big in the frame and I also wanted to exclude much of the surrounding details and concentrate attention on this area where the most striking shapes and textures were concentrated.

Acting

This viewpoint was some distance away and, as I was unable to approach any closer without losing this very pleasing arrangement, I had to use a long-focus lens in order to isolate this area of the scene.

Technical Details
6 x 4.5cm SLR camera with a 300mm lens and 81B warm-up filter on Fuji Velvia.

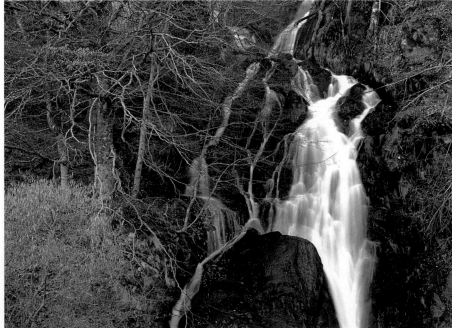

The Valley of Chaudefour near le Mont-Dore in the Auvergne region of France

Technical Details
6 x 4.5cm SLR camera with a 105–210mm zoom lens
and 81A warm-up filter on Fuji Velvia.

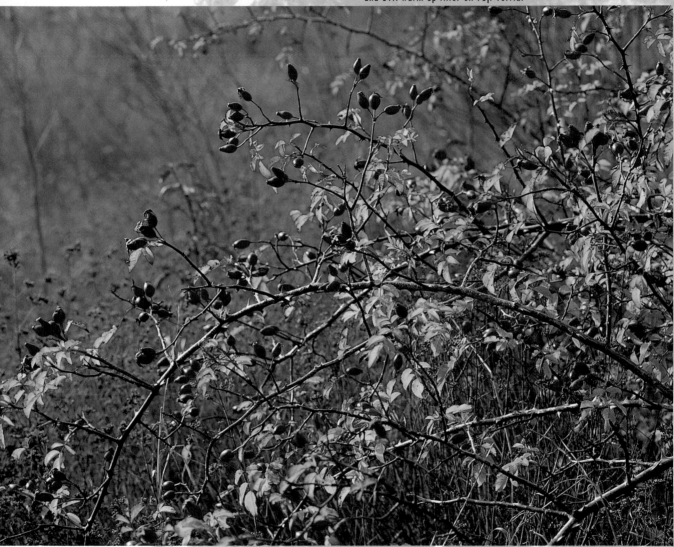

The North Downs near Otford in Kent, UK

This, too, was a winter shot taken on a day with hazy sunlight. I liked the way the soft back-lighting had made the red berries and golden leaves almost seem to leap out from the subdued brown background, creating a bold, colourful effect. I used a long-focus lens to frame a small section of the bush and set an aperture which would give me enough depth of field to record the most important details sharply but leave the background slightly out of focus.

The conditions for good landscape photography when shooting in colour can be quite demanding. Unlike many other subjects, the landscape can easily have a rather bland and ordinary quality which has much to do with the preponderance of blue sky and green foliage in the countryside. Consequently, objects and details which create a contrast with these dominant colours, like a field of sunflowers or a tree displaying autumnal colours, are often the key to producing a striking image.

Seeing

The mountainsides in this region were carpeted by these fields of golden and white plants and I had been looking for a contrasting feature which would help to create a striking composition. I saw this rather small and insignificant tree as I drove along and decided to investigate.

Thinking

From where I first saw the tree it appeared to be almost in the middle of the field and rather lost but as I approached more closely I realised that with a very close and low viewpoint I might be able to make it appear on the horizon where its impact would be much greater.

Acting

I chose a viewpoint which placed the most attractive area of the plants in the immediate foreground and set the camera quite low, almost to the tops of the plants, and as close as I needed to place the tree on the horizon. I used a wide-angle lens to allow me to include as much of the foreground as possible and a good area of the sky. I framed the image so that the tree was not quite on the intersection of thirds.

Reed beds near Priego in Castile Leon, Spain

I was attracted by the three distinct bands of colour in this image with the contrasting red reeds and blue sky being separated by the silvery tree trunks. I used a long-focus lens to isolate the most striking part of the scene and used a polarising filter to increase the colour saturation, with an 81C warm-up filter to give the reds an added boost.

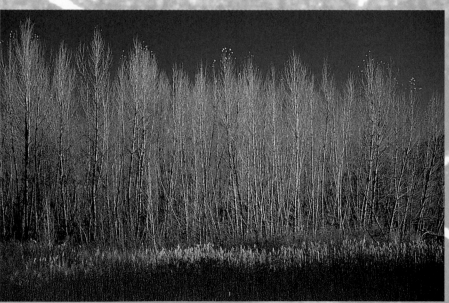

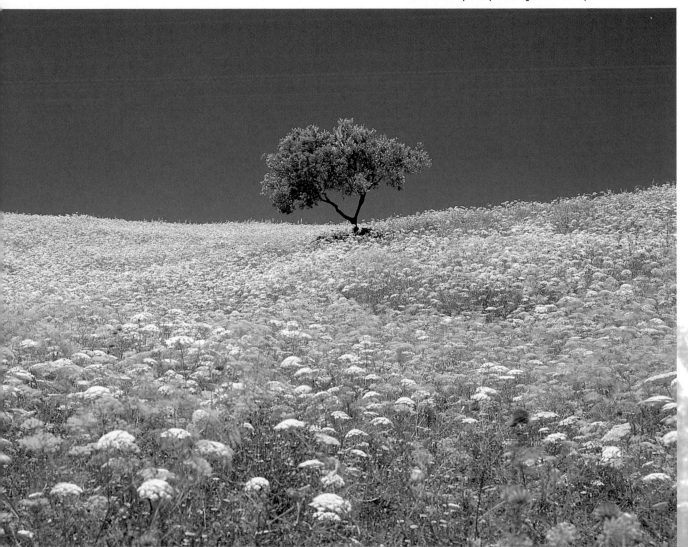

Technical Details
6 x 4.5cm SLR camera with a 55–110mm zoom lens,
81B warm-up and polarising filters on Fuji Velvia.

A spring meadow near Velez Malaga in Andalucia, Spain

Here you can see how much less effective the photograph would have been if it had been taken from a higher and more distant viewpoint, with the tree set against the field instead of the sky.

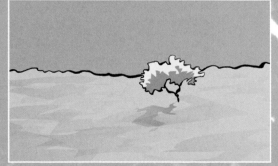

Technical Details
35mm SLR camera with a 75–300mm zoom lens,
polarising and 81C warm-up filters on Fuji Velvia.

Seeing

In the winter the vines are pruned right back to the stumps which reveals this tracery of wires which is set up to support the vines when they are in leaf. Because the wires are very thin and reflective they're not always very visible. But on this occasion, as the sun was going down I could see that, from the right viewpoint, there could be a potentially powerful image.

Thinking

I drove around this area for a while before finding this viewpoint on a slight rise in the essentially flat landscape. It was elevated enough to give me a view of the tops of the wires and for them to reflect the orange sky.

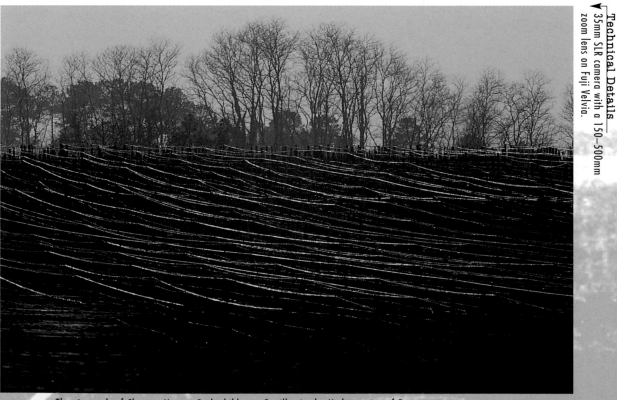

Technical Details
35mm SLR camera with a 150–500mm zoom lens on Fuji Velvia.

The vineyards of Chateau Mouton Rothschild near Pauillac in the Medoc region of France

Acting

I was now quite distant from the area where the effect was strongest. I needed to use the longest setting on my long-focus zoom lens in order to isolate this area and use both the camera's mirror lock and delayed action setting to eliminate the risk of camera shake.

It was the intense greenness which attracted me to this scene. Because I was seeing the sloping olive grove from the opposite side of a small, steep valley I had an almost aerial view of the trees which reduced the image to mysterious patterns of disparate shapes which the monochromatic quality of the image enhanced. I used a long-focus lens to isolate the most effective area of the scene.

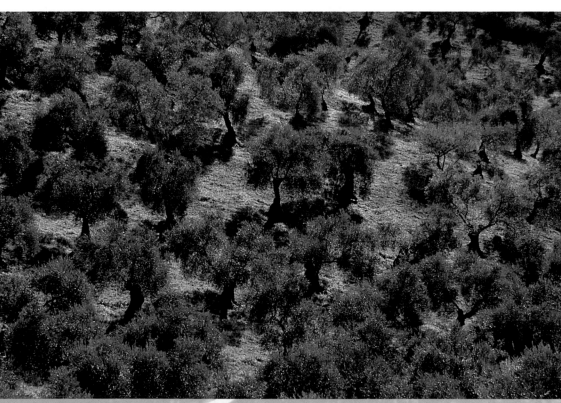

An olive grove near Casares in Andalucia, Spain

Technical Details
35mm SLR camera with a 75–300mm zoom lens, polarising and 81C warm-up filters on Fuji Velvia.

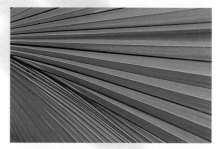

The Art of Composition for
Garden Photography

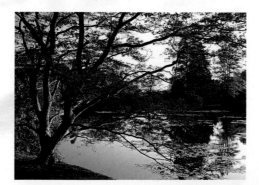

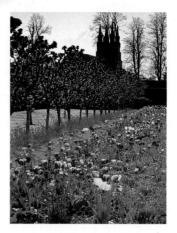

3

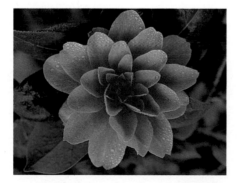

The way in which the main points of interest in a scene are arranged within the viewfinder determines how effective the resulting garden photograph will be. This chapter shows how these key elements can be readily identified and explains the methods you can use to emphasise them.

Choosing a Viewpoint

The choice of viewpoint is central to the composition of an image and one of the most important decisions a photographer must make. When photographing gardens, remember that they have been designed with certain viewpoints in mind. Although this should by no means restrict your choice of camera angles, it is well worth taking into account.

Seeing

This ornate iron screen set into the stone archway caught my eye as I walked towards the rose garden.

Thinking

The garden beyond was in full sunlight and the archway was in shade, and I thought that the **darker foreground shape** would create an effective frame for a picture of the garden, as well as creating a **heightened** sense of **depth**.

Acting

My first thought was to shoot the archway **front-on** so that its shape was symmetrical. But from that viewpoint the pinnacle of the iron screen coincided with the top of the tree and the two details became confused. Also, from here the highlighted statue was right on the edge of the arch and became a distraction instead of a strong feature. I moved a few feet to my right which avoided these two problems and presented a **more pleasing perspective** of the archway.

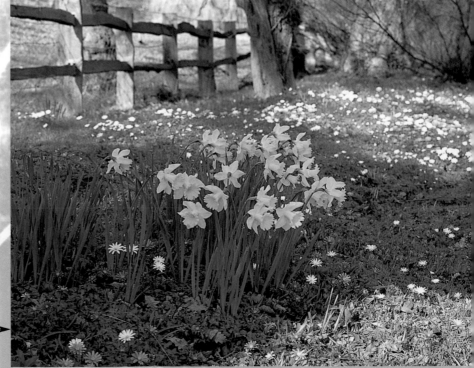

Leeds Castle gardens near Maidstone in Kent, UK

This shot appealed to me as the clumps of daffodils were in a pool of shade and the darker area of grass behind them acted as an effective background, making them seem even brighter. I chose a viewpoint which allowed me to place a section of the rustic wooden fence behind them to add a further element to the composition.

Technical Details

6 x 4.5cm SLR camera with a 105210mm zoom lens and an 81B warm-up filter on Fuji Velvia.

Technical Details
▼ 35mm SLR camera with a 20–35mm zoom lens,
polarising and 81C warm-up filters on Fuji Velvia.

Rule of Thumb

When looking for a viewpoint it's worth looking behind you as well as towards your subject as, in this way, you will sometimes find objects which can be used effectively as foreground interest.

Hever Castle Gardens near Edenbridge in Kent, UK

Here you can see how this subject would have appeared from a more front-on viewpoint.

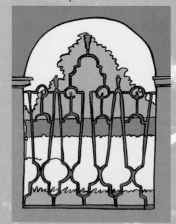

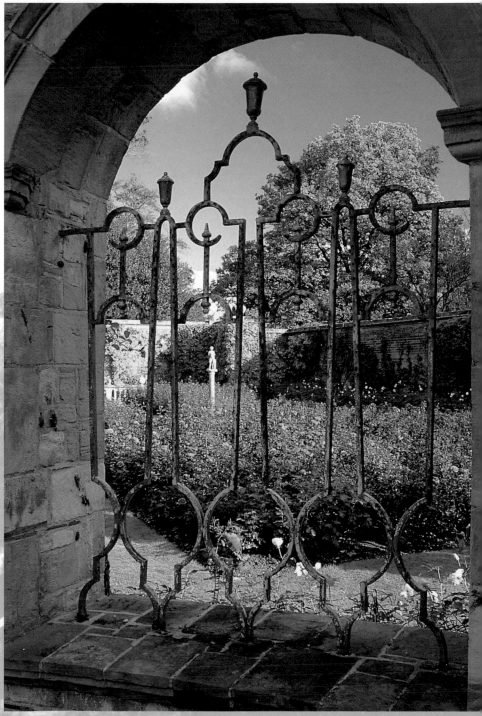

Choosing a Viewpoint

Seeing

These gardens depend for their appeal upon the striking geometric design of the borders, and this was most obvious as I approached them initially from a high viewpoint.

Thinking

I thought that this would be the most effective viewpoint for the picture I wanted and made my first exposure from this position using a wide-angle lens to include as much of the garden design as possible.

Acting

As I walked down the steps towards the garden level I could see how effective a lower viewpoint could also be. Using the same lens from a position close to the edge of the border, the shape created by the exaggerated perspective became quite extreme and the curving pathway produced a strong sense of depth and added a powerful element to the composition. Although this image is less informative about the nature of the garden, and its pattern, I feel that it is more striking graphically.

Technical Details ➤
6 x 4.5cm SLR camera with a 35mm lens and a 81B warm-up filter on Fuji Velvia.

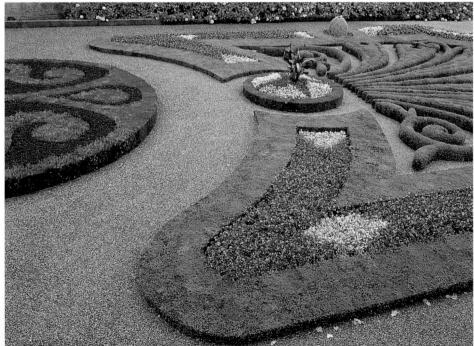

The Gardens of the Palais de la Berbie at Albi in the Tarn, France

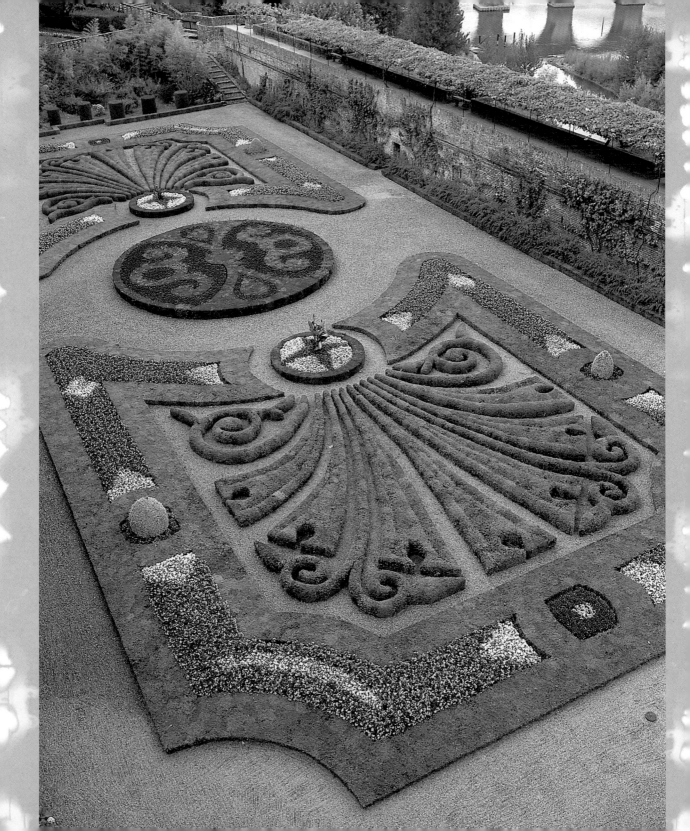

Choosing a Viewpoint

Seeing

The bold contrast between the blue sky and the red of the fuchsias, and the stark, textural quality of the statue were the most dominant features of this scene, shot by Julien Busselle, and he looked at various angles from which these elements would be most strikingly juxtaposed.

Thinking

Julien decided to use a close viewpoint which would enable him to fill the frame with as much colour and texture as possible and, at the same time, would allow him to shoot upwards towards the statue and make use of the sky as a background which has helped to keep the image quite simple and uncluttered.

Acting

To maximise the intensity of the blue sky and to enhance the colour saturation of the fuchsia blooms, Julien used a polarising filter and a small degree of underexposure.

Technical Details
▼ 6 x 4.5cm SLR camera with a 105–210mm zoom lens and an 81C warm-up filter on Fuji Velvia.

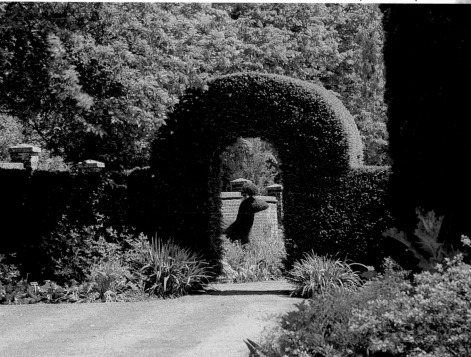

Marle Place, Brenchley in Kent, UK

The viewpoint needed for this picture by Julien Busselle was very precise as the focus of the composition was the curiously shaped topiary framed inside the hedge's archway together with the small splash of red. He framed the shot so that the remainder of the image was restricted to green shapes and textures and used an 81C warm-up filter to counteract the potential blue cast caused by midday summer sunlight.

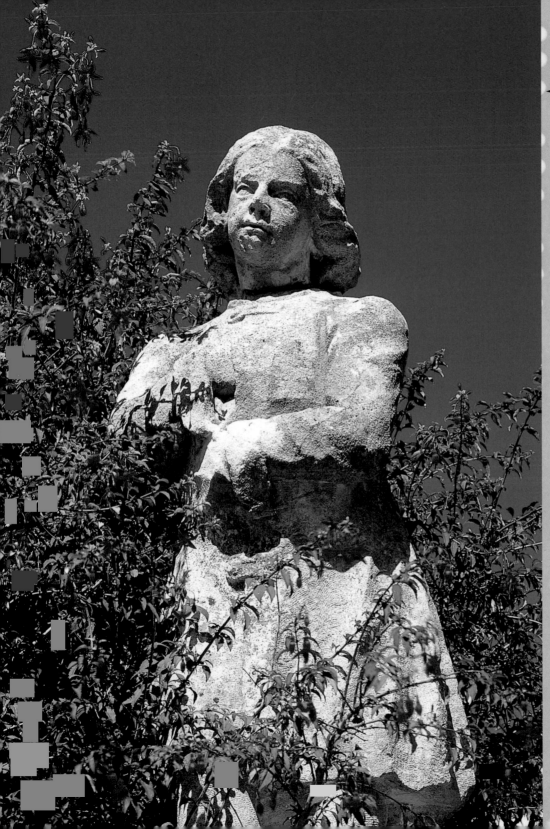

Tapeley Park, Instow in
North Devon, UK

◄ **Technical Details**
6 x 4.5cm SLR camera
with a 55–110mm zoom
lens and a polarising
filter on Fuji Velvia.

Technique
It's important to
appreciate that the
**choice of
viewpoint** will
also affect the lighting
quality of a subject.
Sometimes either this
decision will have to be
a compromise or you
will need to return to a
specific viewpoint at a
**different time
of day** when the
light is directed from a
more effective angle.

Using Shapes & Patterns

All photographs depend for their effect on a number of individual visual elements. The most successful are usually those in which one or more of these elements is boldly and clearly defined. The outline or shape of a subject is the element which usually first identifies it, and a photograph with a dominant shape invariably has a strong initial impact.

Seeing

The vivid colour of these asters created a strong impact which was heightened by the boldly contrasting yellow centres of the flowers. The clump of flowers was quite extensive and unruly and my first attempts to photograph the blooms were hindered by the presence of too many which had passed their best.

Thinking

I realised that I was more likely to produce a pleasing image if I was very selective and framed the image tightly to exclude all but the most pristine blooms. By doing this I was also able to instil a strong sense of pattern and order in the image.

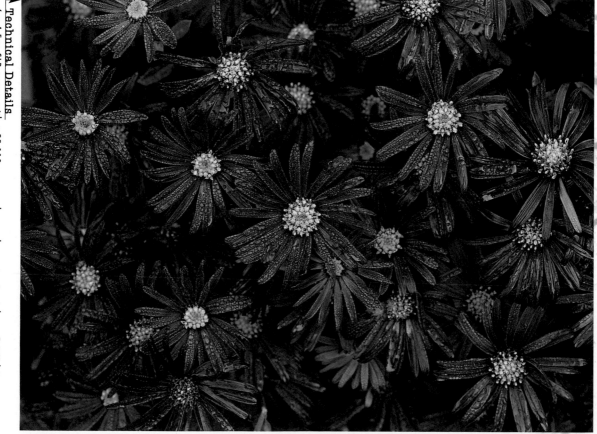

Technical Details
6 x 4.5cm SLR camera with a 55-110mm zoom lens and an extension tube on Fuji Velvia.

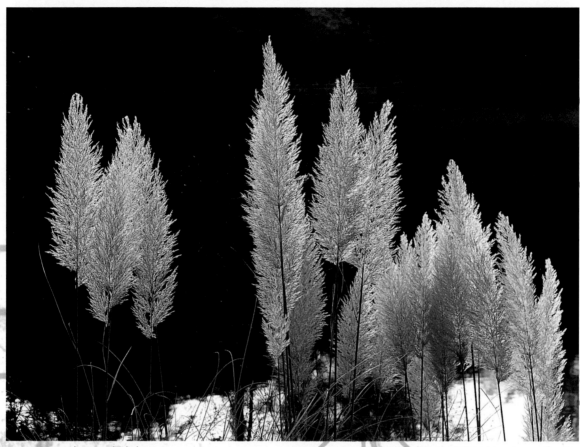

Pampas grass, shot into the light.

I shot this picture of pampas grass directly into the light late on an autumn day which has highlighted their bold shapes against the deeply shaded background. The sun was so low, however, that it created strong lens flare and I had to shield the lens to avoid this problem. I have a useful home-made gadget for this created from a flexible arm, a bulldog clip and a piece of black plastic.

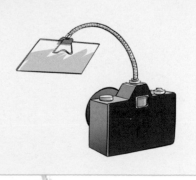

My lens shield device.

Acting

I fitted an extension tube between my zoom lens and the camera which gave me a great deal of flexibility in choosing the distance between the camera and subject and the number of blooms to include in the frame. I set a small aperture of f16 which required a shutter speed of 1/4 second and had to wait until the slight breeze, which was ruffling the flowers, momentarily dropped before making the exposure.

Using Shapes & Patterns

Seeing

Although it was the rich, back-lit colours of the tulips which first attracted me to this scene, I was intrigued by the way the lighting had also created a striking silhouette of the distant village church and the trees surrounding it. The effect of the back lighting on the spring foliage of the fruit trees was also enhanced because they were juxtaposed against the almost-black background.

Thinking

I found a viewpoint which enabled me to place the border in the foreground leading away towards the church and used my zoom lens on a wide setting to include as much foreground as possible.

Acting

I chose a small aperture to ensure that both close and distant details were sharp and used a neutral-graduated filter to help retain some tone in the sky. Shooting into the light made it necessary to use a lens shield to prevent flare.

Technical Details
▼ 35mm SLR camera with a 35–70mm zoom lens and an extension tube on Fuji Velvia.

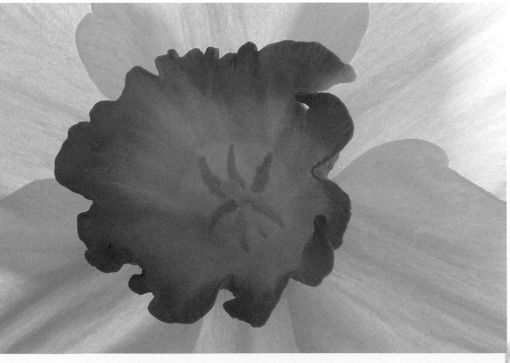

Close-up shot of a daffodil

I was struck by the bold shape the orange centre of this daffodil created against the paler yellow of its petals, which the strong back lighting emphasised, and decided to make this the main feature of the shot. I used an extension tube to allow me to focus closely enough to exclude all but the petals from the image and used a small aperture to ensure adequate depth of field.

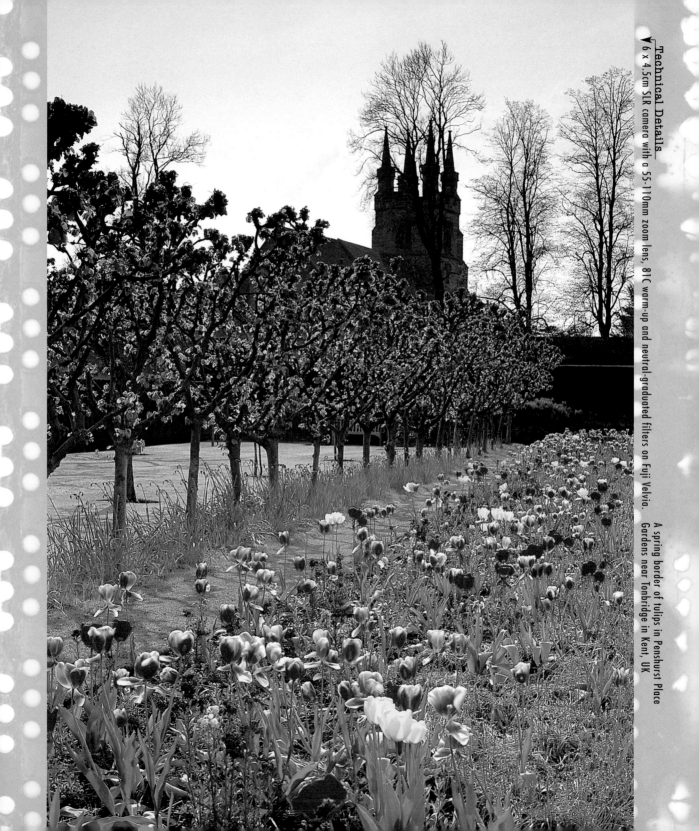

Technical Details
6 x 4.5cm SLR camera with a 55-110mm zoom lens, 81C warm-up and neutral-graduated filters on Fuji Velvia.

A spring border of tulips in Penshurst Place Gardens near Tonbridge in Kent, UK

Emphasising Texture

The medium of photography is especially effective at conveying an impression of texture, a quality which can be particularly powerful in subjects like gardens and flowers. Texture is the form within an object's surface. It needs the subtleties of an image's tonal range to reveal it effectively and is largely dependent upon the direction and quality of the light.

Seeing

I saw this gnarled tree as I walked along the edge of a wood late on an autumn afternoon. The low-angled sunlight was glancing along its surface, revealing a very tactile texture, while the warm glow of the late sun enhanced the rich colour of the bark.

Thinking

I wanted to keep the image as simple and direct as possible and decided to frame the shot tightly, excluding details of the woodland behind and allowing only the brown bark and black background to be included in the frame.

Acting

I chose a viewpoint which created the most striking lighting effect and which also placed a featureless area of shaded background behind the tree. Then I used my zoom lens to adjust the framing in the way I wanted.

Technical Details

▼ 6 x 4.5cm SLR camera with a 105–210mm zoom lens and an extension tube on Fuji Velvia.

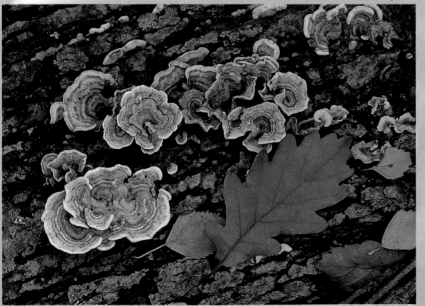

Tree fungi

This arrangement of autumn fungi on the trunk of a fallen tree depends for its appeal upon a limited colour range and the contrasting textures of the bark, leaves and fungi. To emphasise this, I opted to frame the image very tightly using an extension tube to allow close focusing. The soft light of the shaded wood was ideal as the textures are quite subtle and strong – directional sunlight would have created excessive contrast with bright highlights and dense shadows. I used a small aperture to ensure adequate depth of field.

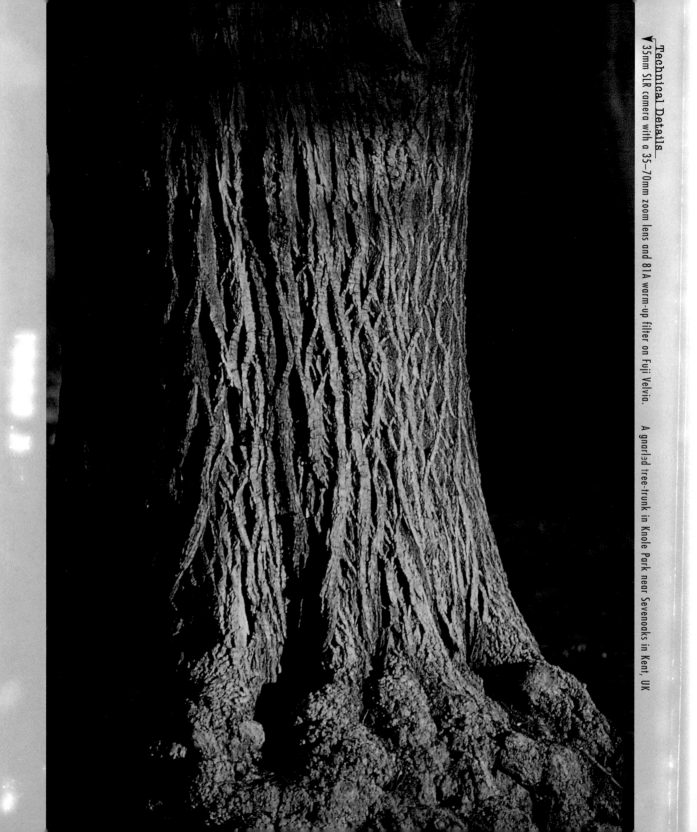

Technical Details
▼ 35mm SLR camera with a 35–70mm zoom lens and 81A warm-up filter on Fuji Velvia.   A gnarled tree-trunk in Knole Park near Sevenoaks in Kent, UK

Emphasising Texture

Technical Details
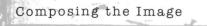
6 x 4.5cm SLR camera with a 55–110mm zoom lens and an extension tube on Fuji Velvia.   My back garden, Kent, UK

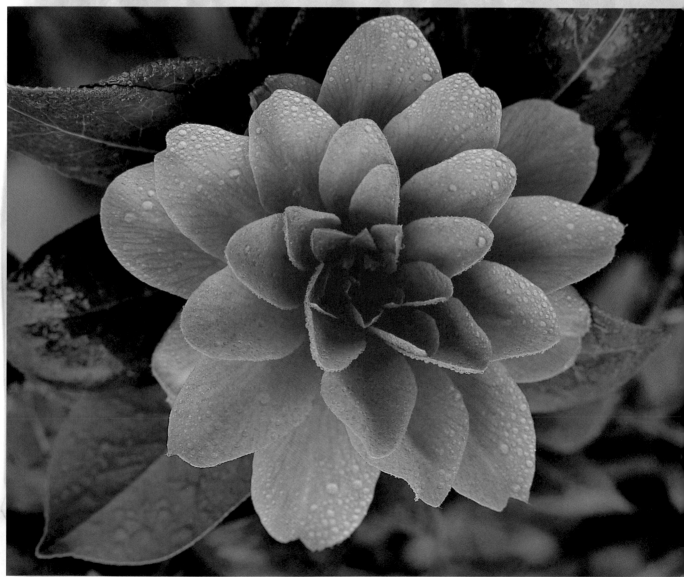

Rule of Thumb

When shooting subjects very close up with an SLR mounted on a tripod, it can help to use the camera's mirror lock to avoid vibration and loss of sharpness, especially when using very slow shutter speeds.

Technical Details
▼ 6 x 4.5cm SLR camera with a 105–210mm zoom lens, polarising and 81B warm-up filters on Fuji Velvia.

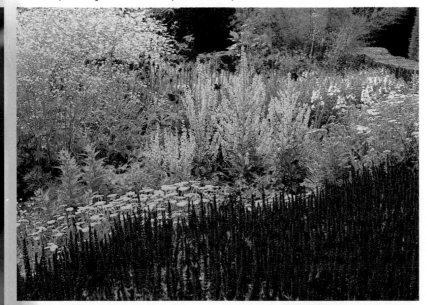

Great Dixter in East Sussex, UK

This shot of a border of salvia and pelargoniums by Julien Busselle has a pronounced textural effect partly because of the way the colours of the individual flowers and leaves are distributed and partly through the way in which the light has created highlights and shadows. He used a long-focus lens to frame a small section of the border quite tightly and set a small aperture to obtain maximum depth of field. He used a polarising filter to keep the colours saturated and a warm-up filter to prevent a blue cast.

Seeing

This camellia bush is in my garden and I had been watching it bloom for some days. On this particular morning there were a number of near-perfect blooms and the shaded sunlight was creating a very pleasing effect, giving an almost luminous glow.

Thinking

I looked at a number of blooms with a view to taking a single, close-up image and some, although otherwise ideal, were simply in a position or angled in such a way as to make it impossible to obtain a good view of them.

Acting

This one proved to be the most suitable flower but I needed to have the camera up quite high. I also pulled the bloom down a little with some thread and moved a couple of unwanted details from the background in the same way. The water droplets were a cheat, added with the aid of a fine plant spray. I felt this enhanced the textural and tactile quality of the image and was not unnatural, as earlier in the morning there had been some dew on the blooms.

Framing the Image

There is a widely-quoted rule of composition that the image should be framed so that the main point of interest is placed where lines dividing the image into thirds intersect. While this will, in most cases, produce a pleasing effect, it should not be followed slavishly – it is important to consider the overall balance of the image before deciding on the way it is framed.

Seeing

This attractive old timbered farmhouse would make an appealing picture at the best of times but when I passed it on this occasion the sunlight was falling on it at a perfect angle and the sky behind was a beautifully clear blue.

Thinking

I felt that the pathway lined with roses and lilies leading towards the door would provide an ideal foreground and help to create a sense of depth in the image. I also felt that the image might well provide a suitable cover for the brochure I was illustrating.

Technical Details
▼ 6 x 4.5cm SLR camera with a 105–210mm zoom lens and a 81C warm-up filter on Fuji Velvia.

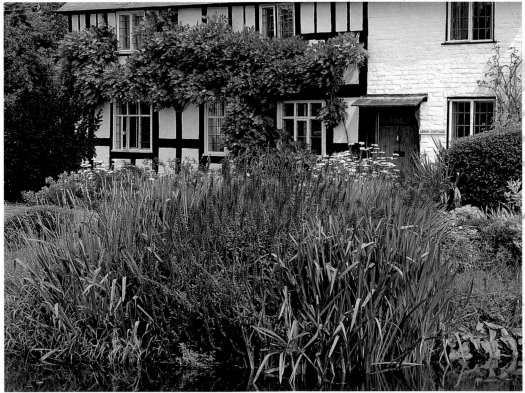

A cottage in the village of Eardisland in Hereford and Worcester, UK

I framed this image quite tightly using a long-focus lens because I wanted to maximise the effect of the colourful display of salvia on the river bank in front of the cottage and the attractive timbered façade. Also the sky was rather pale and milky and would have detracted from the image.

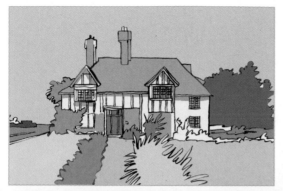

Notice how much more effective the image is when composed in an upright format than as a horizontal (landscape).

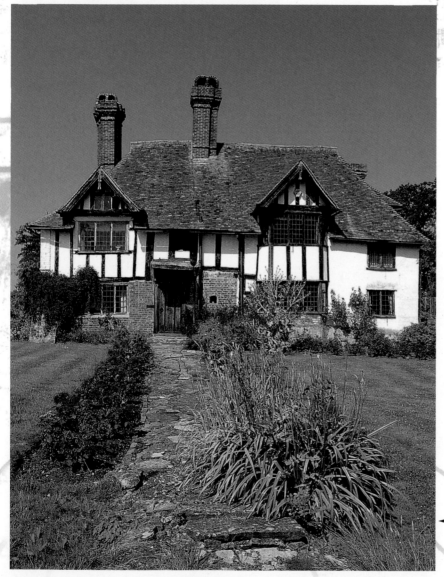

Acting

I chose a viewpoint from where the path led **directly away** from the camera and turned the camera to an **upright format**, framing the image to include as much of the foreground as possible, as well as a good area of the **blue sky** which might be used for a **headline**. I used a **polarising filter** to increase the colour saturation of the blue sky and an 81C warm-up filter to counteract the potential **blue cast** created in midday summer sunlight and with a deep blue sky.

Rule of Thumb

By far the majority of photographs taken with 35mm cameras are in landscape format. This is often simply because it is easier and more comfortable to hold the camera in this way, although quite often an upright shape would provide a more pleasing composition. It can help to make a habit of always looking first at a potential picture with the camera held upright to be sure of not overlooking this possibility.

A farmhouse near the village of Pluckley in Kent, UK

Technical Details

6 x 4.5cm SLR camera with a 50mm wide-angle lens, polarising and 81C warm-up filters on Fuji Velvia.

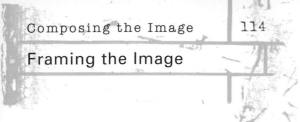

Technical Details
▼ 35mm SLR camera with a 20–35mm zoom lens, polarising and 81C warm-up filters on Fuji Velvia.

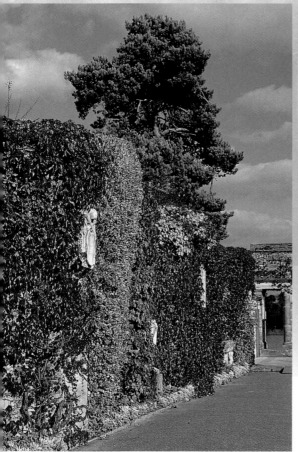

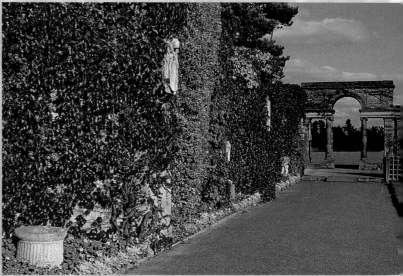

Hever Castle Gardens near Edenbridge in Kent, UK

These two photographs, taken from the same viewpoint, demonstrate how strikingly the composition of an image can be changed by the simple action of switching from a landscape to an upright format. Although the archway is lost in the upright shot, I feel it works better as the inclusion of the tree creates a more dynamic shape. I used a polarising filter to increase the colour saturation of the image.

Seeing
The distant white bench reflected in the lake became the focus of attention for Julien Busselle in this scene, while the darkgreen tones which dominate the image gave it an added drama.

Thinking
Julien decided to include the foreground flowers which introduced another colour and helped to lead the eye towards the bench.

Technical Details
▼ 6 x 4.5cm SLR camera with a 55–110mm zoom lens on Fuji Velvia.

Marwood Hill near Barnstaple in North Devon, UK

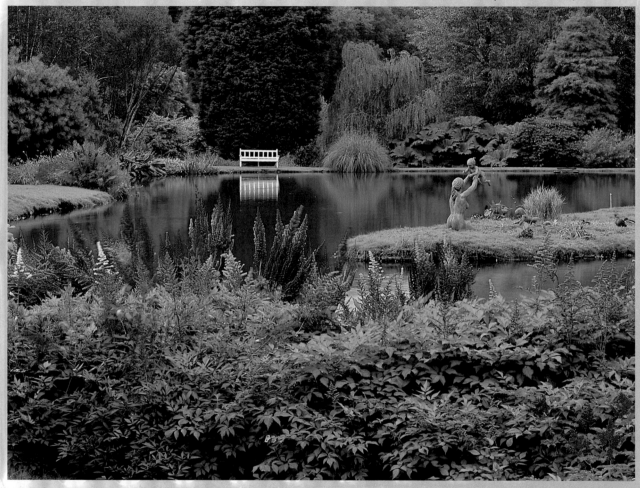

Acting

He chose a **viewpoint** which placed the mass of flowers in the gap created by the green lakeside bank and framed the shot using his **zoom lens.** Then he **angled the camera** so that the bench was placed just **off centre** on a line about one-third of the way from the top of the frame.

Rule of Thumb

When deciding how best to frame a shot it is first necessary to identify the main focus of attention in the scene. This will help you decide how much more of the scene needs to be included and where the most effective place for this key detail will be within the image.

Using Perspective

Perspective is the effect created by the diminishing size of objects as they recede from the camera, as you can see looking down a tree-lined avenue, for instance. It's a valuable way of helping to give an image a sense of depth and distance and also contributes to the impression of solidity and the three-dimensional quality which a photograph can have.

Seeing

It was almost impossible not to react to the deep red leaf colour of this autumnal acer, but I was also attracted to the silhouetted trees on the far shore of the lake and their reflections in the water.

Thinking

In normal circumstances I try to avoid featureless, pale skies in colour landscape photographs like this but I realised that a combination of the deep red foliage, the white sky and black silhouetted trees could be quite powerful.

Acting

I decided to use a wide-angle lens which would enable me to get very close to the tree and fill the frame with the colour of its leaves but, at the same time, allow me to include a large area of the sky, lake and opposite bank. This, in turn, has given the image of strong sense of depth and distance. I felt that the exposure might be a problem as the large area of bright sky could result in underexposure, so I bracketed quite widely to be safe. In the event, I preferred a slightly underexposed frame to that which was indicated.

Rule of Thumb

The effect of perspective varies according to the relative distances between the camera, the nearest objects and those furthest away. If the image includes both foreground and distant objects the perspective effect will be marked, so that, for instance, a group of flowers nearby can appear much larger than a distant tree. But if there is no immediate foreground and all the principal objects are some distance away from the camera there will be a minimal suggestion of perspective and objects will be shown close to their true relative size.

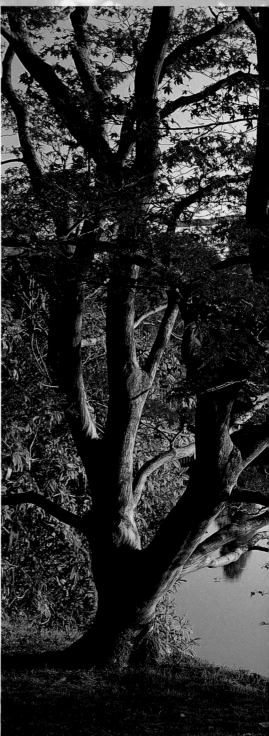

The main lake in Sheffield Park Gardens near Lewes in Sussex, UK

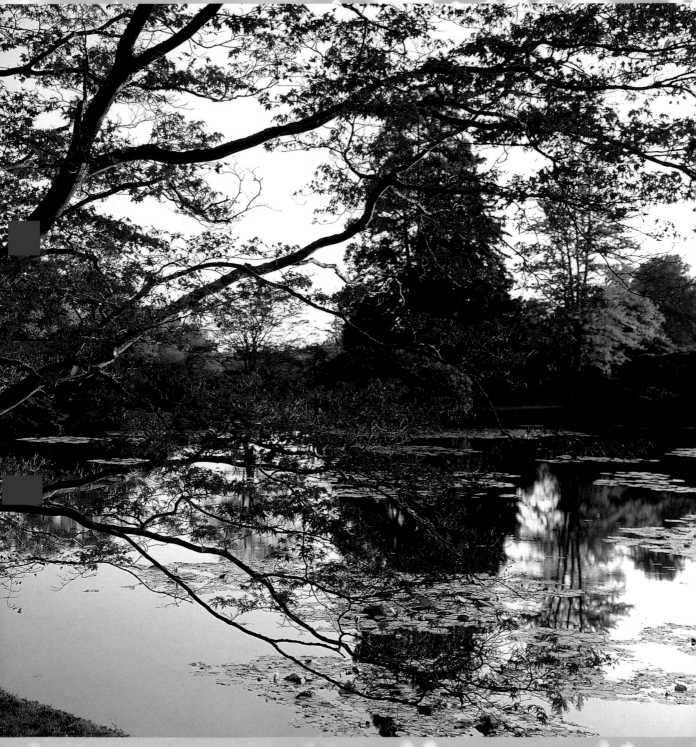

Technical Details
▼ 6 x 4.5cm SLR camera with a 50mm lens and a 81C warm-up filter on Fuji Velvia.

Seeing

The dense planting of lavender and nicotiana in this scene created a very striking mixture of colour and texture, and I spent a while looking for a viewpoint which would combine these details in the most telling way.

Thinking

I felt that the most effective way of exploiting the qualities of colour and texture would be to use the perspective effect to compress the details of the scene. I was also aware that the image needed an additional, contrasting detail to give the composition a positive focus of attention.

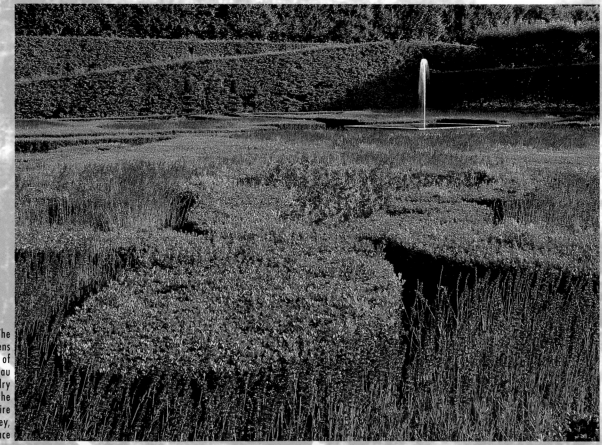

The Gardens of Chateau Villandry in the Loire Valley, France

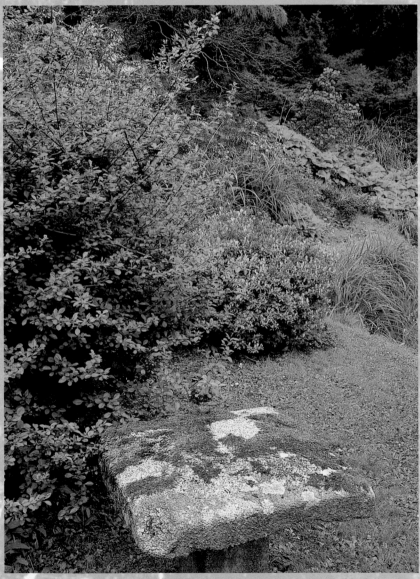

Powerscourt Gardens near Wicklow in County Wicklow, Eire

This moss-covered stone seat provided a good counterpoint to the mass of
flowers and green foliage behind it and added an essential element of
contrast and interest to the shot, as well as helping to create a more
three-dimensional quality in the photograph. I framed the shot so that
the light tone of the seat and the splash of purple blooms were in
opposite corners of the image and used a small aperture to ensure that
both the seat and distant flowers were in sharp focus.

Acting

This viewpoint allowed me to include the
fountain as the key element and also,
happily, created the most pleasing
lighting quality, shooting
towards the late afternoon sun. I used the
longest setting on my zoom lens to
isolate a fairly small area of
the scene, cropping out the sky, and used
the smallest aperture to obtain maximum
depth of field. I needed to use
my lens shield device to prevent flare.

Technical Details
6 x 4.5cm SLR camera with a 55–110mm zoom
lens and a 81C warm-up filter on Fuji Velvia.

Technical Details
6 x 4.5cm SLR camera with a 105–210mm zoom
lens and a 81C warm-up filter on Fuji Velvia.

Colour & Design

Most photographers react enthusiastically to colourful subjects, and gardens provide an abundant source. Paradoxically, very colourful subjects can be the most difficult to photograph successfully unless a restrained approach is adopted. As a general rule, it is best to limit the dominant colours in an image to just two or three. Often pictures which are almost monochromatic are the most striking in colour photography.

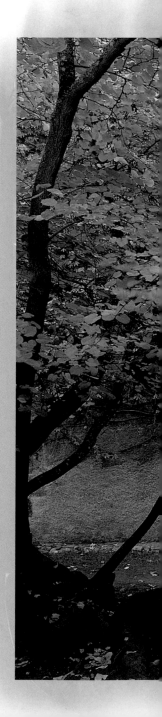

Seeing

The vivid autumnal colour of the boston ivy above the blue stable doors was hard to overlook as a potential picture, and my first instinct was to shoot a fairly close-up image of these two details.

Thinking

The two colours were so strong that I decided to use them smaller in the image as a focus of attention rather than as the main feature of the image.

Acting

I found a more distant viewpoint which allowed me to include the tree in the foreground when I fitted my wide-angle lens and, although it introduced another colour, the striking contrast between its green foliage and the two smaller splashes of vivid colour seemed to enhance them all.

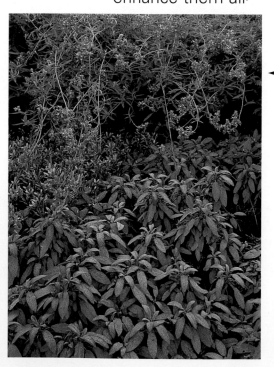

Technical Details ➤
6 x 4.5cm SLR camera with a 55–110mm zoom lens and a 81C warm-up filter on Fuji Velvia.

◄ **Technical Details**
6 x 4.5cm SLR camera with a 55–110mm zoom lens on Fuji Velvia.

The very limited colour range of this clump of sage appealed to me, together with the texture and pattern created by the leaves. I decided to frame the shot quite tightly to exclude any other details. The picture was taken in the open shade on a late sunny afternoon with a blue sky, and in normal circumstances I would have used a warm-up filter to counteract the potential blue cast. However, I felt the colour cast might enhance the monochromatic effect I wanted and shot the picture without a filter.

The Chateau of Georges Sand in the village of Nohant in Berry, France

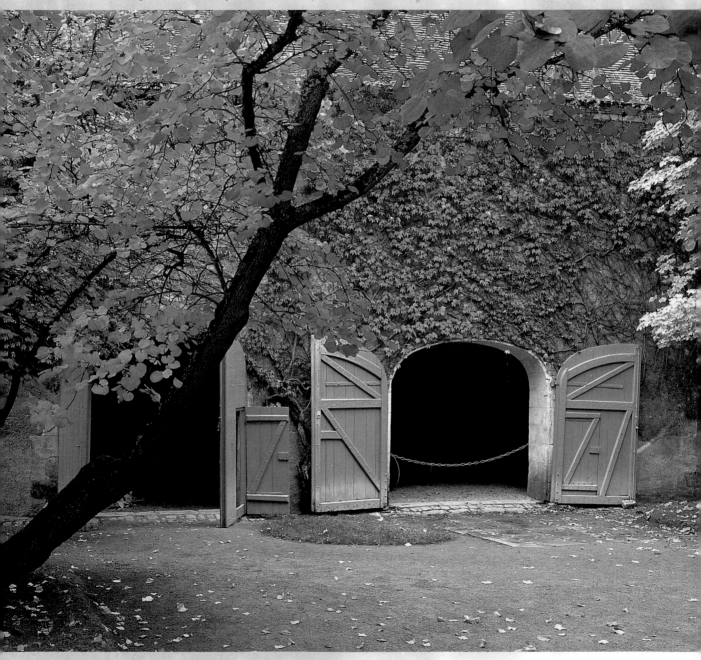

Colour & Design

Rule of Thumb

Very colourful subjects are often much more effective when photographed in soft, diffused daylight such as on a hazy or overcast day or in open shade on a sunny day. Direct sunlight can create too many bright highlights and shadows which dilute the effect of bold colours, creating far less impact.

Seeing

This border of scarlet tulips presented one of those situations where it is easy to lose the **striking effect** of the colour because of the presence of **too many** others.

Thinking

I felt that my best option was to shoot a **close-up** image of just a few blooms. But there was a danger that the brick-wall **background** might still be too **distracting**.

Acting

I decided to use a fairly **distant viewpoint** and frame my image tightly with a long-focus lens, selecting just two blooms. I used a **wide aperture** to limit the depth of field which has resulted in the brick wall being very soft and **unobtrusive** and provided a sympathetic foil for the red tulips.

Technical Details

▼ 35mm SLR camera with an 80-200mm zoom lens and a 81B warm-up filter on Fuji Velvia.

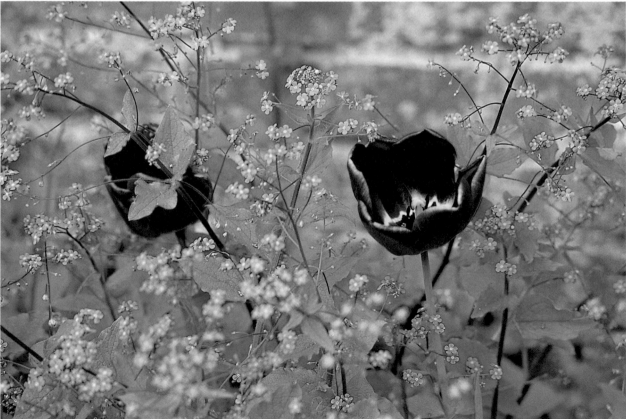

Garden in Kent, UK

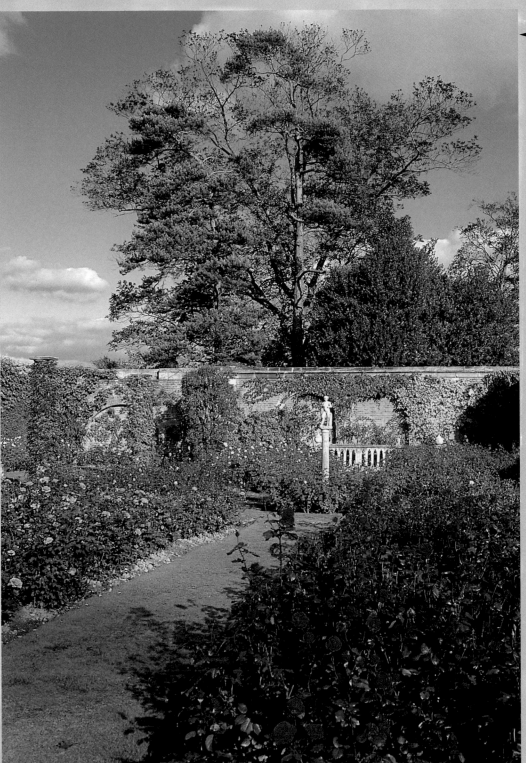

Technical
Details
35mm SLR camera
with a 120–35mm
zoom lens,
polarising and 81C
warm-up filters on
Fuji Velvia.

The rose garden at
Hever Castle near
Edenbridge in Kent,
UK

Scenes like this can
easily not work well
as a colour
photograph because
there are too many
conflicting colours. In
this case the very
bright colour of the
roses in the
foreground has been
subdued because they
are partially shaded.
If they had been in
full sunlight I feel the
image would not have
been so pleasing. I
used a polarising
filter to increase the
density of the blue
sky and the colour
saturation of the
blooms.

Close-up Photography

Moving much closer to plants and flowers can often reveal details of astonishing beauty. Close-up photography can highlight shapes and patterns in natural forms which wouldn't otherwise be visible and give them an importance and impact far beyond their scale.

Seeing

I'd noticed this ivy-covered stone wall from some distance away and had, in fact, shot some pictures from a distance of about two metres. The colour of the stone and green leaves made an effective composition along with the contrasting textures.

Thinking

I'd also noticed the small patches of lichen but they were rather lost in the larger-scale view I'd taken, so I moved in much closer to take a better look. I realised that there was, perhaps, a more striking picture to be had by isolating a very small area of the wall.

Acting

The leaves in this shot, taken from only 30cm or so away, are very small. By closing in like this, I was able to find a spot where the leaves were similar in size to the patches of lichen and managed to combine them in a way which created a nicely balanced composition. I used a small aperture to ensure adequate depth of field.

Technical Details ➤
35mm SLR camera with a 90mm macro lens and 81A warm-up filter on Fuji Velvia.

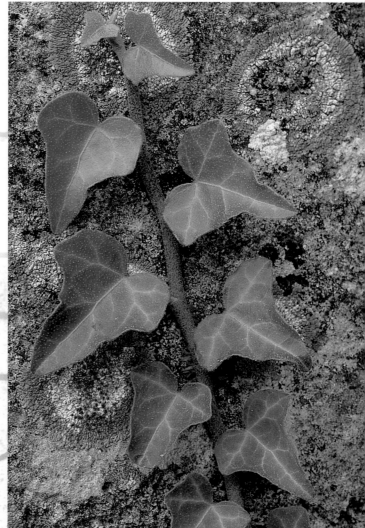

Stone wall near Matlock in Derbyshire, UK

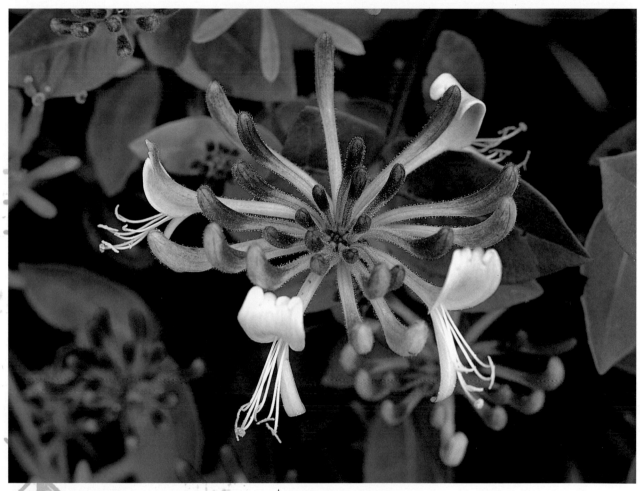

Close-up shot of honeysuckle

This honeysuckle bloom was photographed in a Devon
hedgerow on a very dull, overcast day when the soft
lighting was ideal to record the subtle texture and colours.
I used a small aperture to obtain sufficient depth of field.

▲ Technical Details
6 x 4.5cm SLR camera with a 55-110 zoom lens and an extension tube on
Fuji Velvia.

Technique

Most cameras have lenses which will only focus down to a couple
of metres or so, but for close-up photography it's often necessary
to come in much closer. Extension tubes or a bellows
unit can be fitted between an SLR camera body and a normal lens
to accomplish this, but a macro lens can be a good
investment for those interested in producing this type of image as
it can create a life-size image of a subject on the film.

Technical Details
▼ 6 x 4.5cm SLR camera with an 80mm macro lens on Fuji Velvia.

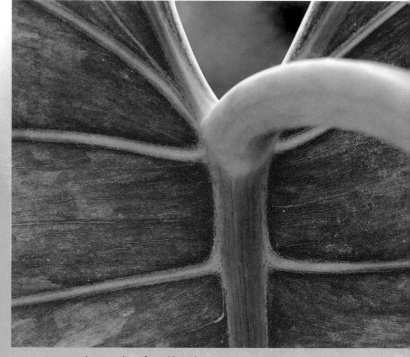

Gardens of Chateau Le Roche Courbon near Saintes, in the Charante region of France.

The strong side lighting has created a strong sense of shape and texture in this shot of a yucca plant by Pat Busselle. The dark-toned background has helped to throw the blooms into strong relief and created an image with considerable impact.

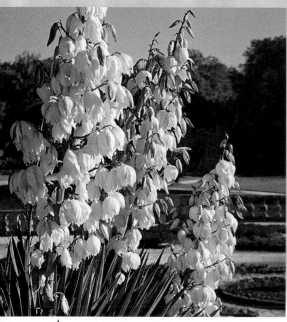

Extreme close-up shot of a rubber plant

This shot of a dying rubber plant leaf was taken from a distance of only about 30cm using a macro lens. The viewpoint and framing were chosen to create an almost abstract quality in which the stem and the back-lit veins of the leaf have created dominant lines.

↑ Technical Details
35mm SLR camera with a 28–35 zoom lens on Fuji Super G 200.

Technical Details →
35mm SLR camera with a 35-70 zoom lens and an extension tube on Fuji Velvia.

Technique

When photographing close-ups of plants and flowers in situ using small apertures, it's often necessary to use slow shutter speeds. This can be a problem when there is even slight wind movement. A useful technique is to erect a small protective screen on the windward side of the subject.

Close-up shot of a palm leaf

Isolating a small section of this palm leaf and framing it so that the veins create diagonal lines has produced an image with a strong graphic quality which the lack of other colours has emphasised.

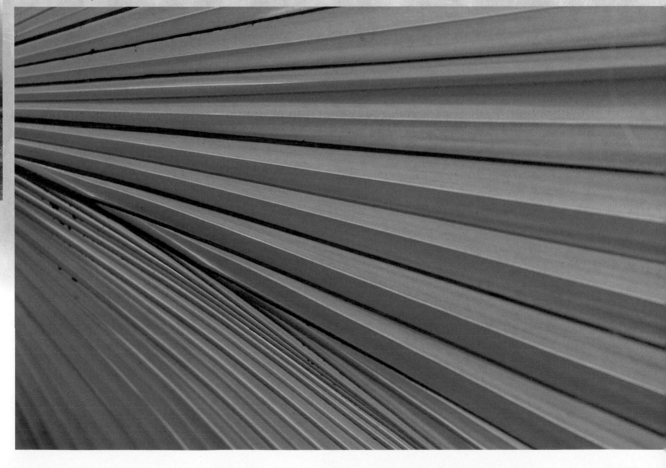

Light & the Landscape

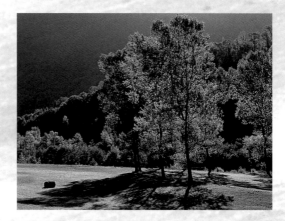

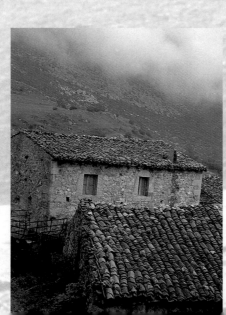

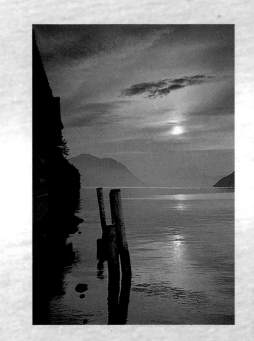

4

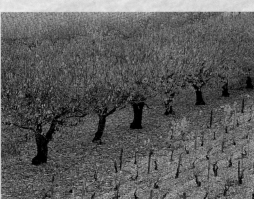

The relationship between light and the landscape is
one which has fascinated countless photographers since the medium was invented and its
effects can be both subtle and dramatic within the space of seconds. This chapter demonstrates
how to be aware of the often fleeting effects which are created and
how to record them successfully.

While a bright sunny day is by no means essential for successful landscape photography, it is on these occasions that most keen photographers are tempted to venture forth with their cameras. But strong sunlight can produce unattractive effects if some care is not taken over the choice of viewpoint and the way the image is framed. This can be especially true of very bright summer days when the sky is a deep blue and there are no clouds to soften it or to reflect light into the shadows.

Seeing

It was a beautiful December afternoon as I travelled through this valley. The warm-toned, sharply angled sunlight was enhancing the colour of the rust-red bracken as well as creating well-defined shadows and revealing a rich texture. Above the mountain-top the sky was a clear, deep blue.

Thinking

My first thought was to choose a viewpoint and frame the image so that an area of blue sky was included. In fact I did so, and the result was quite pleasing but I felt that in some ways this had detracted from the powerful effect which the sunlight had created on the bracken.

Acting

I decided to change my viewpoint slightly which enabled me to include the trees at the bottom of the picture and to frame the image more tightly. This meant that the sky was excluded and the emphasis was placed more strongly upon the effects of the sunlight.

The valley of the River Duddon in Cumbria, UK

Technical Details
6 x 4.5cm SLR camera with a 105–210mm zoom lens, 81B warm-up and polarising filters on Fuji Velvia

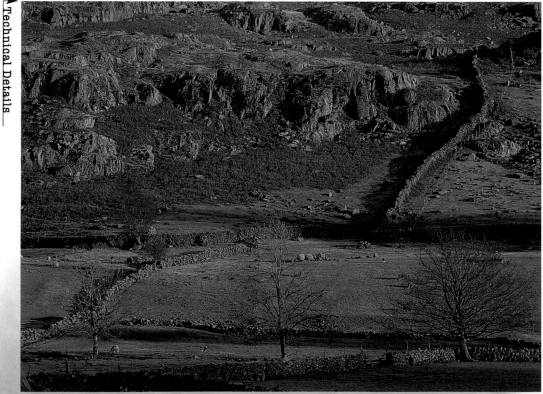

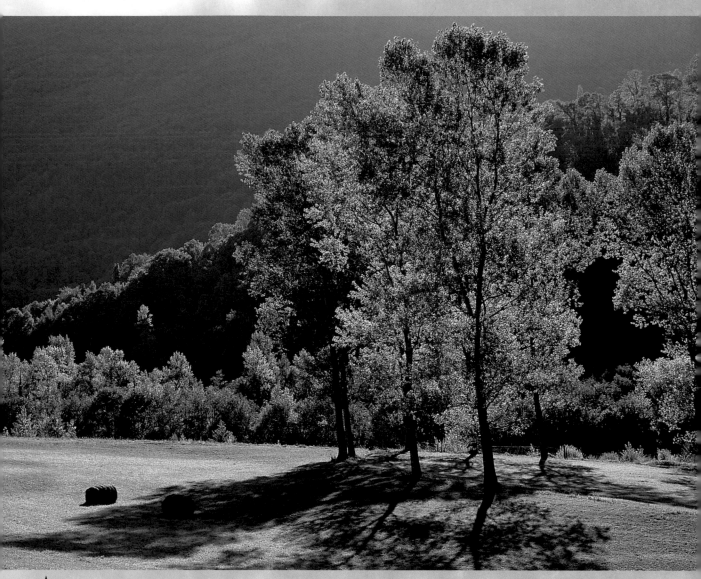

Technical Details
6 x 4.5cm SLR camera with a 105–210mm zoom lens
and 81B warm-up filter on Fuji Velvia.

Near Lourdes in the Hautes Pyrenees region of France

It was late afternoon when I saw this scene in a narrow Pyrenean valley and I was
attracted by the effect which the back-lighting had created as I looked towards this
group of trees. In order to retain the dramatic quality of the lighting I needed to
frame the image so that the mountain-top and pale sky were excluded, allowing the
dark, shaded mountainside to create a bold contrast with the highlighted trees.

Technique
The right level of contrast is very important in colour
photography. Too little and the image will appear flat
and lacking in colour saturation, too much and the
photograph will be harsh and unappealing and the
subtlety of the colours will be lost.

Seeing

I was immediately attracted by this beautifully shaped lone tree with a deep blue sky behind it. But from the position where I first saw it, the very strong sunlight was creating a quite harsh quality with half the tree in deep shadow and the other half very brightly lit.

Thinking

I decided to walk around the tree to see if a change in the viewpoint and the corresponding change in the angle of the lighting would improve its effect. As the tree was almost symmetrical, a change in viewpoint had little effect on its shape but the lighting quality improved dramatically.

Acting

I used a low camera angle to ensure the tree trunk was placed against the sky and not the grass, and used a polarising filter to maximise the colour saturation of both the sky and the green leaves.

The Sierra de Cazorla in Andalucia, Spain

Technical Details
35mm SLR camera with a 35–70mm zoom lens, 81C warm-up and polarising filters on Fuji Velvia.

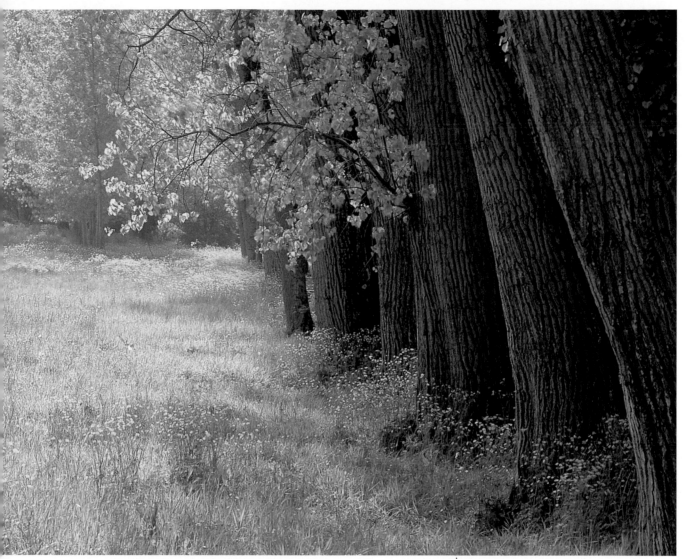

Near Coulon in the Marais Poitevin region of Deux Sèvres, France

Because this was a very hazy day, when the sunlight was soft and created little contrast, I was able to choose a viewpoint and frame the image in such a way that I could include almost equal amounts of shadow and highlighted areas without the image appearing too contrasty.

Technical Details
6 x 4.5cm SLR camera with a 55-110mm zoom lens and 81B warm-up filter on Fuji Velvia.

Technique

It can help you to judge the contrast of a scene by viewing it through half-closed eyes or through the viewfinder of an SLR camera with the lens stopped down.

Rule of Thumb

Although the subject itself, combined with the angle and quality of light, are primarily responsible for establishing the contrast of an image, a considerable amount of control can be achieved by the choice of viewpoint and the way in which the image is framed.

The Time of Day

The time of day can have a considerable effect on the quality and mood of a photograph. In the middle of the day the sun reaches its highest peak and the shadows are at their smallest. The colour quality of the light at this time is also at its bluest. Earlier and later in the day the light has a much warmer quality and the shadows lengthen. Also, of course, during a day in high summer the angle of the sun in relation to a particular view changes by almost 180 degrees.

Seeing

This dramatic outcrop of red rock overlooking the bay of Porto is a famous Corsican landmark but like many such places it can be hard to photograph in a way which captures something of its astonishing colour and rugged character.

Thinking

Finding a good viewpoint was not very difficult – in fact, I saw this from the roadside on the outskirts of the village and it proved to be one of the most impressive aspects of the site. However, I felt that, lit in the normal way, the rocks would not have the impact I hoped to achieve.

Acting

I planned to return later in the day, towards sundown, to see if at this time the angle of the light would create strong relief as well as accentuating the rich colour of the rock. To my delight both of these things occurred and the sun set at an angle which allowed me to leave it until the very last moment before shooting which has produced this almost unreal colour with very pronounced contours and texture.

Les Calanches near the village of Piana in Corsica

▲ **Technical Details**
35mm SLR camera with an 80–200mm zoom lens on Fuji Velvia.

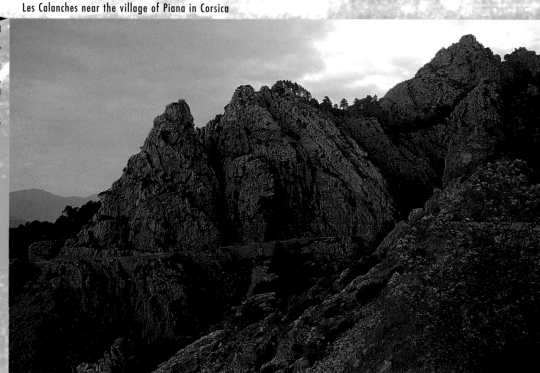

The River Dordogne seen from the village of Domme in the region of Aquitaine, France

This viewpoint is one of the best from which to photograph the river Dordogne and is very easy to find. In order to produce an image with a more subtle and interesting colour quality, I simply got up very early to shoot the scene just before the sun came up and while there was still some mist lingering in the valley.

Technical Details
▼ 35mm SLR camera with an 80–200mm zoom lens on Fuji Velvia.

Seeing

I came across this wintry scene in the early afternoon on a day when the sun was strong and the sky quite clear. In open countryside, this lighting would have probably produced an image with only a small amount of shadow and little contrast but here, with the steep contours and bare trees, it created almost too much contrast.

Thinking

I liked the rich texture the lighting had produced and felt that if I could find the right viewpoint I would be able to use the hard lighting to good effect.

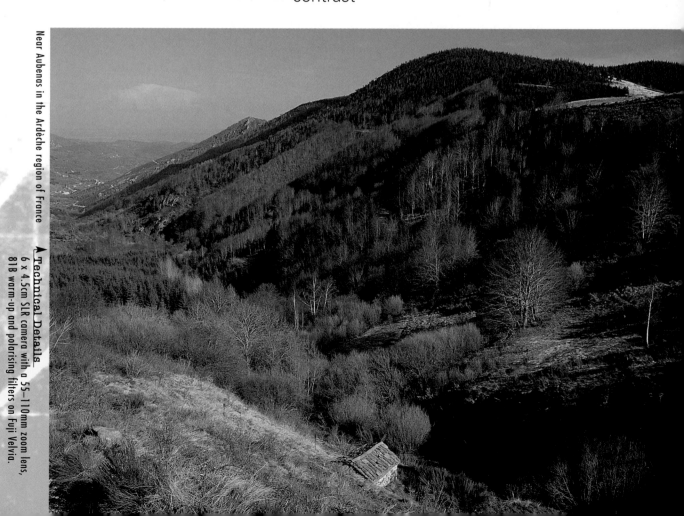

Near Aubenas in the Ardèche region of France

▲ Technical Details
6 x 4.5cm SLR camera with a 55–110mm zoom lens,
81B warm-up and polarising filters on Fuji Velvia.

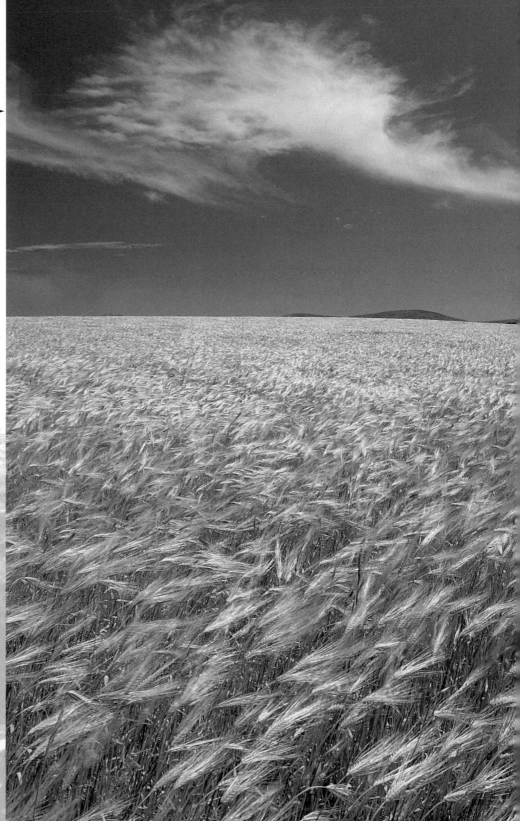

Technical Details ➤
35mm SLR camera with a
20–35mm zoom lens,
81C warm-up and polarising
lens on Fuji Velvia.

Acting

I found that from this **viewpoint** I was able to bring a little of the near slope into the foreground together with the small stone hut which helped to give the image a sense of **depth and distance**. By framing the image quite tightly I was also able to exclude some of the deepest area of shadow and throw more emphasis on to the highlighted trees on the right of the image in a way which seemed to create a pleasing balance overall.

A wheat field near Avila in Castile Leon, Spain

I saw this beautiful field of ripe, golden corn as I was driving along a country road in the middle of the day. The overhead sunlight was creating only very small shadows and the conditions for normal landscape shots were not ideal. But this lighting had created a very pleasing, shimmering quality on the ears of wheat and the presence of the strong blue sky and white cloud added the necessary degree of contrast and interest.

Shooting on Cloudy Days

A warm, sunny summer's day is the sort of occasion most photographers would choose when planning a day's landscape photography. But a cloudy or overcast day can still create very pleasing effects and even bad weather conditions, such as fog, frost and stormy skies, can give an image an instant eye-catching quality and create a degree of interest and impact which can be lacking in the more bland light of a perfect sunny day.

Seeing

It had been a clear sunny day but as I climbed into the mountains a dense, low cloud enveloped the landscape, reducing visibility to only a hundred metres or so. But there were occasional glimpses of trees and rocks which made me feel that, with the right subject, I might well be able to produce an interesting photograph.

Thinking

As I approached a small hamlet, the bright red tiled roofs of these two barns almost seemed to light up the road and made an ideal subject to set against the murky background.

Acting

I found a slightly raised viewpoint which enabled me to look down on the nearest roof and to fill the foreground with colour. I framed the shot tightly to make the most of the red tiles and also to exclude some distracting details at the sides.

Technical Details
▼ 6 x 4.5cm SLR camera with a 55–110mm zoom lens on Fuji Velvia.

Near Potes in the Picos de Europa, Cantabria, Spain

Taken on a similarly murky day, this barn is much further from the camera than the previous picture and its colour is very muted, but its shape has become very dominant through the mist. This alone would not have interested me but the nicely placed tree beside it made the image work for me and the small window added interest to the shape of the barn.

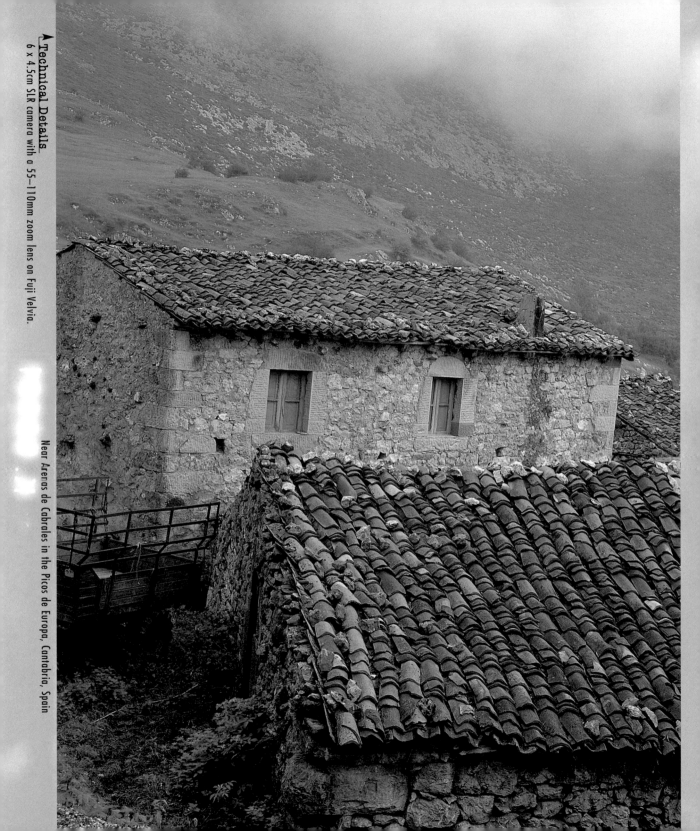

Technical Details
6 x 4.5cm SLR camera with a 55–110mm zoom lens on Fuji Velvia.

Near Areras de Cabrales in the Picos de Europa, Cantabria, Spain

Seeing

This shot was taken on a late October day when the sky was heavily overcast and it was raining. The scene was very softly lit but I was attracted by the misty background, the subtle colour of the autumn leaves and the water.

Thinking

I realised that the problem would be insufficient contrast and that the image could easily be flat and uninteresting and looked for a way in which I could overcome this.

Acting

I found this viewpoint which placed the overhanging branches of a tree very close to the camera. Being silhouetted, they added a considerable amount of contrast to the image as well as increasing the sense of depth and distance and they also helped to create a more interesting composition. I used a small aperture to ensure both the foreground branches and more distant details were recorded sharply.

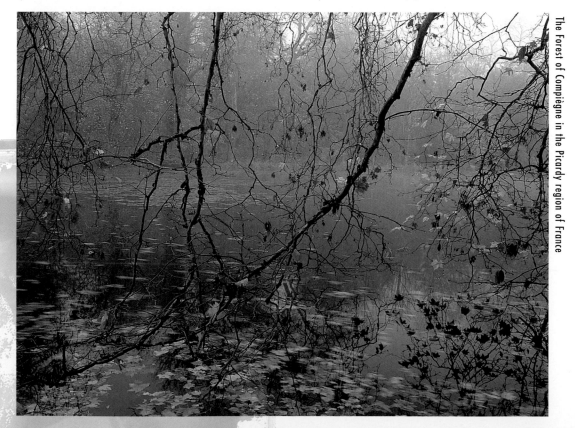

The Forest of Compiègne in the Picardy region of France

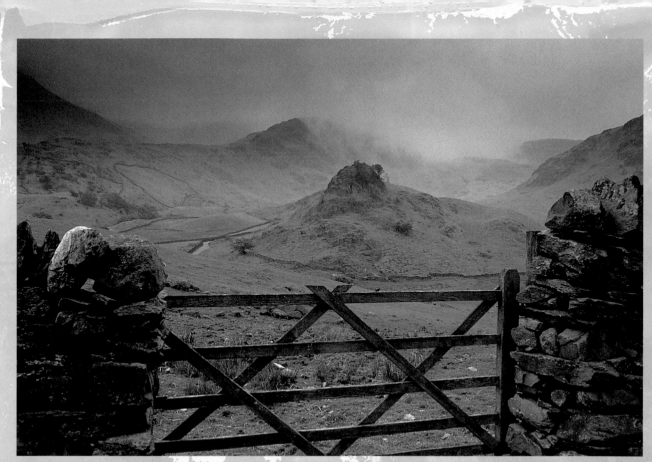

Wrynose Pass in Cumbria, UK

It was a very murky day in winter with very poor visibility as I travelled over this pass and there appeared to be very little chance of an interesting photograph. But this old farm gate and dry-stone wall provided the essential element of foreground contrast and I was able to use a neutral-graduated filter to reduce the sky exposure to reveal some interesting tone and colour.

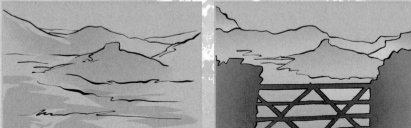

See how the impact of the image has been increased by the inclusion of dark foreground details.

Technical Details
35mm SLR camera with a 24mm lens and 81b warm-up on Fuji Velvia.

Technical Details
6 x 4.5cm SLR camera with a 55–110mm zoom lens and 81B warm-up filter on Fuji Velvia.

There are few photographers who can resist the temptation of a spectacular sunset or sunrise, and staying up late and getting up early are two of the best ways of increasing your chances of taking pictures which stand out from the crowd. As well as the more dramatic qualities of sunrises or sunsets, dusk and dawn can create some quite subtle and beautiful effects, even on a cloudy day. But some care is needed if your photographs are to capture the stunning effects you see before you as the brightness range of scenes like these is often beyond the range of colour films unless you take steps to control it.

Seeing

This is a very beautiful beach, about seven miles long, but with very few interesting features along the coastline or shore. For this reason I felt my best chance of a striking photograph would be at sunset, as it had a westerly outlook.

Thinking

I arrived about half an hour before the sun was due to set and walked along the shore looking for a viewpoint where the incoming waves were making a nice shape. I decided to use a wide-angle lens and a viewpoint which allowed the surf to come up almost to the camera.

Acting

I waited until the sun was weakened by its proximity to the horizon, and by passing clouds, and then made a series of exposures over a period which extended until sometime after it had set. The resulting images were extremely varied in both colour and quality – these two pictures were taken within only about ten minutes of each other.

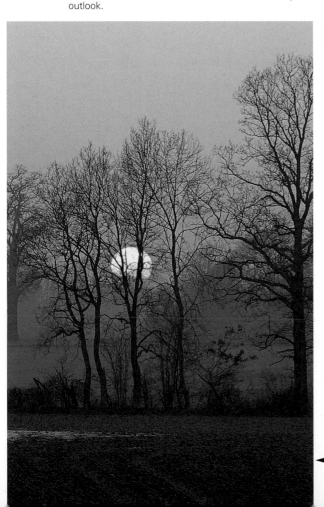

The Darent Valley near Tonbridge in Kent, UK

I'd been looking for a location from which I might be able to shoot a large sun setting close to the horizon and which had something of interest in the foreground. This large flat meadow with a pleasingly shaped group of trees in the distance seemed ideal and the presence of some lingering snow added a further element of interest.

◄ Technical Details
35mm SLR camera with a 150–500mm zoom lens on Fuji Velvia.

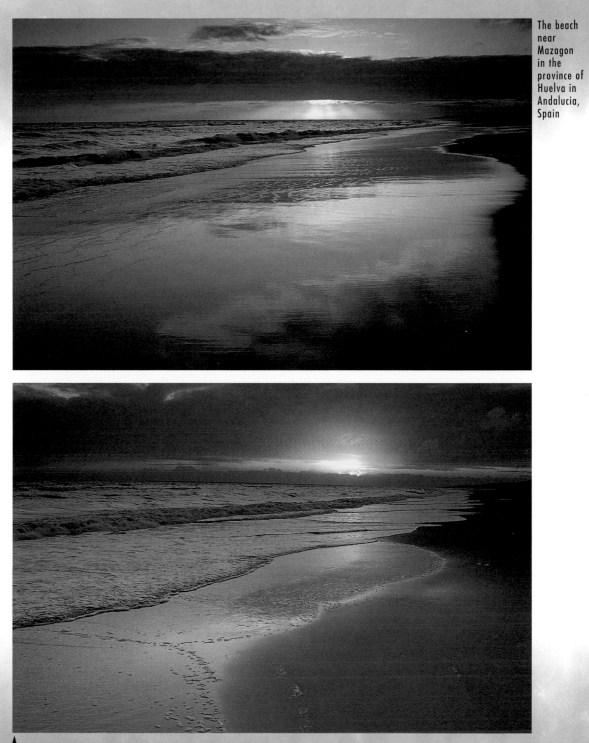

The beach near Mazagon in the province of Huelva in Andalucia, Spain

Technical Details
35mm SLR camera with a 20–35mm zoom lens on Fuji Velvia.

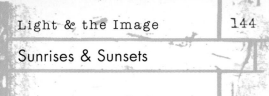
Thinking

I found this small group of trees and decided I would **wait** to see if the sun might break through, setting up my camera, choosing my **viewpoint** and **framing** the image in readiness.

Seeing

I woke in my hotel on this morning to find that the view from my window was completely obliterated by a **dense fog**. But as I travelled higher on to the moor I could see that the sun was only quite thinly veiled in places and thought that if it became just a little bit stronger there might well be the possibility of a good picture.

Acting

My efforts were rewarded when this sudden clearing in the fog allowed the sun to filter through casting this delicious **golden light** over the scene. I used a **neutral-graduated filter** to help even the balance between the very bright sky and the darker foreground.

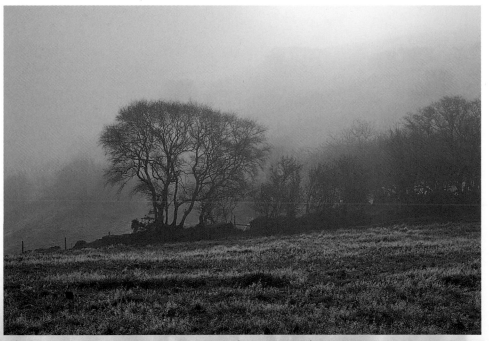

Exmoor near Combe Martin in North Devon, UK

Victoria Falls, Zimbabwe

I wanted to go home with an interesting photograph of this famous site, and in normal daylight hours, although it looked mightily impressive, I felt that it needed another element to help capture its remarkable drama on film. Lighting quality is often the factor which lifts an image from the ordinary so I decided to arrive at this spot in time for sunrise. I had to shoot the picture very quickly after the sun appeared over the falls as it gained strength very rapidly and soon became too bright to record on film. I used a neutral-graduated filter to help weaken it further.

Technical Details
35mm SLR camera with a 20–35mm zoom lens on Fuji Velvia.

Technical Details
35mm SLR camera with a 35–70mm zoom lens and neutral-graduated filter on Fuji Velvia.

Rule of Thumb

It helps to know precisely where to go when planning to shoot a sunrise or sunset. Getting up at 4 am and then driving round looking for something to photograph is a recipe for frustration and disappointment. When travelling around I like to keep a look out for possible locations with interesting foregrounds, using a compass to establish where the colourful sky is likely to be.

Light & Texture

The medium of photography is especially effective at conveying an impression of texture and this can be a powerful element in landscape photography, both in distant views and with more close-up images. The effect of texture is largely dependent upon the direction and quality of the light in relation to the nature of the surface it illuminates. In a distant landscape, acutely angled sunlight, such as that of late afternoon, might be necessary to reveal this quality but with a closer image, such as a detail of rocks or trees, a softer, more frontal light is likely to be more effective.

Seeing

It was a wintry afternoon with a quite weak sun when I saw this outcrop of rock. I was taken by its shape but also by the wonderfully textural quality which the angled sunlight had created.

Acting

I chose a viewpoint which presented the most pleasing aspect of the rock and also placed the bright part of the cloudy sky in the most effective juxtaposition with it. I decided not to use a warm-up filter as I felt the resulting blue cast might contribute to the atmosphere of the photograph.

Thinking

The sun was at such an acute angle that had it been a clearer day, and the sunlight any stronger, the image would have simply been too contrasty and the textural quality greatly diminished.

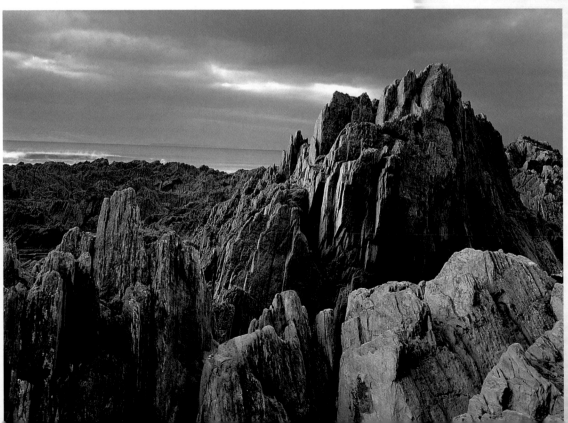

Barricane Beach near Woolacombe in North Devon, UK

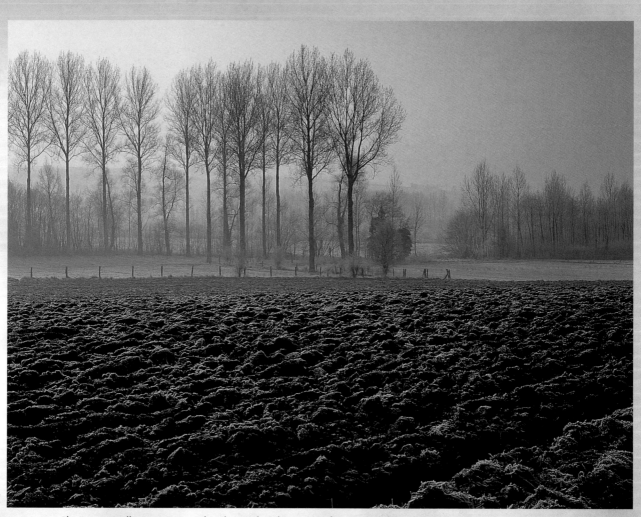

The Ternoise Valley near Montreuil in the Pas-de-Calais region of France

I saw this scene very early on a winter's morning when a hoar frost had carpeted the landscape. The combination of the newly ploughed field with its deep furrows and the highlights created by the frost and the low-angled sunlight skimming across the field has produced an image with a very striking impression of texture.

Rule of Thumb

Creating a strong impression of texture needs the image to be critically sharp and it's best to use a slow, fine-grained film, select a small aperture to ensure adequate depth of field and use a tripod to eliminate the risk of camera shake.

Technical Details
6 x 4.5cm SLR camera with a 55–110mm zoom lens and neutral-graduated filter on Fuji Velvia.

Technical Details
6 x 4.5cm SLR camera with a 55–110mm zoom lens on Fuji Velvia.

Technique

When using a long-focus lens to isolate a small area of a distant view it's advisable to mount your camera on a tripod and use a cable release as the effect of camera shake will be magnified. When using an SLR camera, one with a mirror lock can be a big advantage as it will eliminate the risk of vibration which is caused when the mirror flips up at the time the exposure is made.

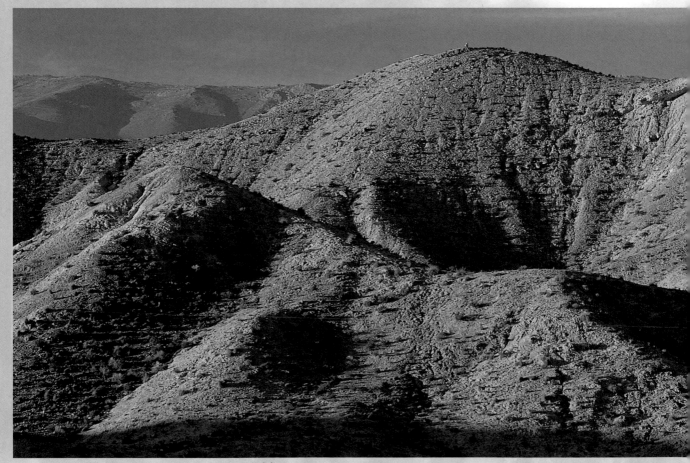

Near Tabernas in the province of Almeria in Andalucia, Spain

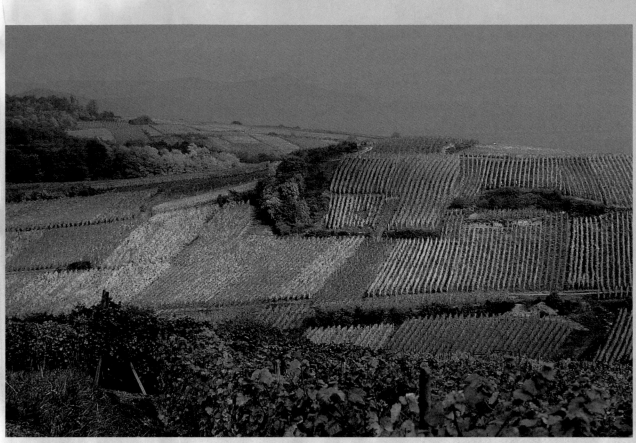

Vineyards near Colmar in the Alsace region of France

The effect of the low-angled evening sunlight on these autumn vineyards created a very strong impression of texture which was enhanced by the rich, warm monochromatic quality of the image. I used a long-focus lens to isolate the most striking section of the landscape.

Seeing

This is a very bleak and barren landscape, where many of the Spaghetti Westerns were made. It is almost treeless and has few features which can be introduced to add colour or other compositional interest to the image.

Technical Details
35mm SLR camera with a 75–300mm zoom lens on Fuji Velvia.

Technical Details
35mm SLR camera with a 75–300mm zoom lens, 81B warm-up and polarising filters on Fuji Velvia.

Thinking

I'd seen this viewpoint as I'd driven along a quiet country road earlier in the day and felt that at a different time, when the sun was at a lower angle, it might create a much more interesting image.

Acting

I was very pleased to find on returning, towards the end of the afternoon, that the sun was now creating quite striking contours and textures and its much warmer colour quality had added a richness to the terrain which now produced a bold contrast against the blue sky. I used a polarising filter to accentuate this and a warm-up filter to enhance the warm quality of the soil.

Light & Colour

The colour quality of daylight varies considerably according to the position of the sun in the sky and factors like cloud and blue sky. In the middle of a summer's day, when there is a deep blue sky, the light can be much bluer than the film is balanced for and also when shooting subjects in open shade and on a cloudy, overcast day. This will create a blue cast on transparency film. Conversely, early morning and late afternoon sunlight can be much yellower than the film is balanced for and this can create a warm colour cast.

Rule of Thumb

When considering whether or not to use a warm-up filter it's worth bearing in mind that, for normal sunlit landscapes, a blue colour cast is invariably less attractive than when the image is a little too warm.

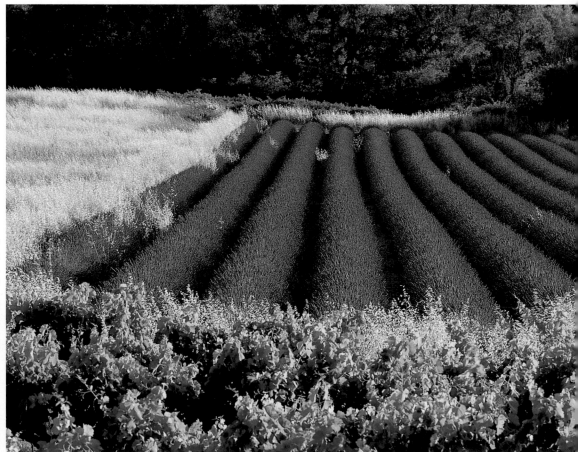

A lavender field near Gordes in the Luberon region of Provence, France

I chose a viewpoint which allowed me to shoot along the rows of lavender and into the light, which helped to create the rich colour and texture of this image, and I framed the shot to include some of the contrasting foreground details.

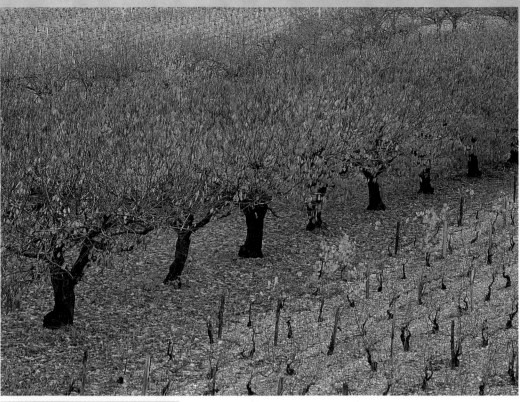

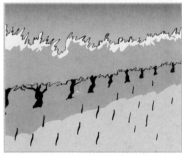

See how including more of the scene in the image and making the diagonal line less dominant would have lessened its impact.

Seeing

It was a cloudy, overcast day in November when I chanced upon this scene. I was immediately struck by the vivid colour of the leaves on the cherry trees, which was enhanced by the soft lighting and by the orderly way in which they were planted which created a strong pattern.

Thinking

I thought that my image needed a stronger sense of shape and design, so I looked for a more distant, raised viewpoint which also gave me a side view of the trees and allowed me to include some of the adjoining vineyard in the foreground.

Acting

I used a long-focus lens to exclude all but the most important details in the scene and framed the shot so that the line of trees created a diagonal in the frame. I used a polarising filter to increase the colour saturation of the foliage and a warm-up filter to make the red leaves look even stronger.

Technical Details
6 x 4.5cm SLR camera with a 105–210mm zoom lens, polarising and 81B warm-up filters on Fuji Velvia.

Technical Details
6 x 4.5cm SLR camera with a 55–110mm zoom lens, 81B warm-up and polarising filters on Fuji Velvia.

Light & Colour

Seeing

I had been skirting the lake shore looking for the possibility of an interesting photograph when I discovered a small jetty near these two weathered mooring posts which I thought could provide effective **foreground interest**.

Thinking

It was late afternoon on a hazy day and I noticed that the **light** had a rather pleasing **bluish** quality which created an **atmospheric** effect and, together with the curious cloud formation, I felt that this might be enough to provide the extra interest I felt the image needed.

Acting

I chose a viewpoint which allowed me to place the two poles at more-or-less the **intersection of thirds** and well-balanced with the lightest part of the sky and then framed the shot to include part of the foreshore. I used a neutral-graduated filter to balance the brightness of the sky with its reflection in the water.

This shows how the impact of the photograph would have been lessened had the image not been cropped so tightly.

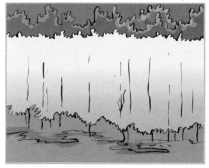

The valley of the River Tajo near Cuenca in Castile La Mancha, Spain

I was driving through this small valley in late afternoon on an autumn day and as the road climbed out of it I saw this scene where the back-lighting had created an almost spot-lit effect on the small tree plantation. I also liked the fact that the tips of the trees had remained green. I framed the shot tightly to restrict the image to just two colours and to exclude the sky. I used polarising and warm-up filters to increase the colour saturation.

Technical Details

 6 x 4.5cm SLR camera with a 55–110mm zoom lens, 81B warm-up and polarising filters on Fuji Velvia.

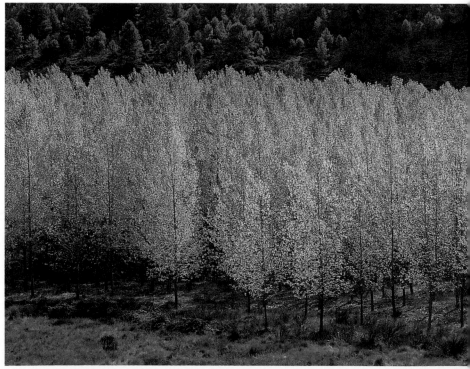

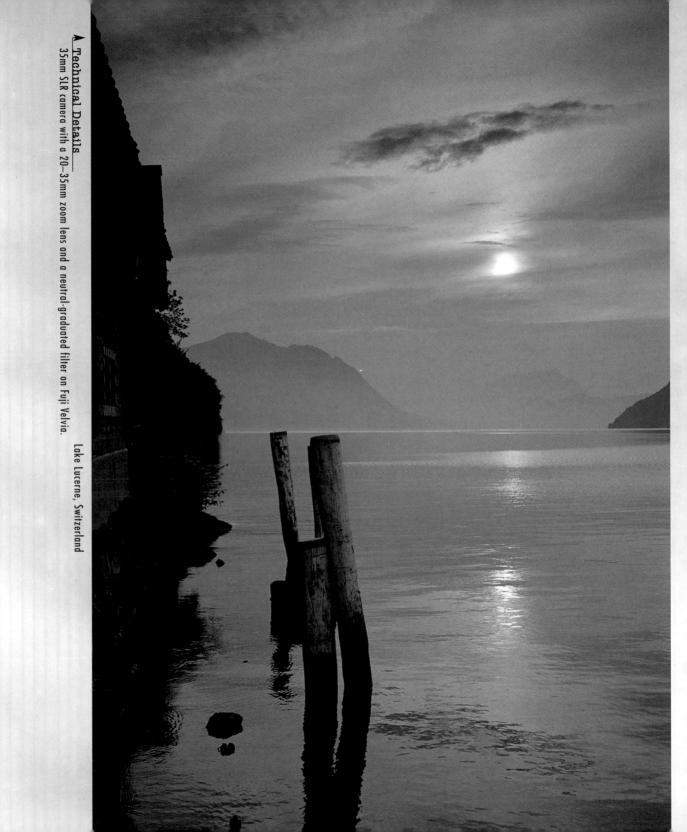

▲ **Technical Details**

35mm SLR camera with a 20–35mm zoom lens and a neutral-graduated filter on Fuji Velvia.

Lake Lucerne, Switzerland

Light & Mood

Mood is an elusive element in a photograph – it's something which can often be present in a situation but it is very difficult to convey on film. Light, colour and mood are closely linked – the blues and greens which dominate the landscape tend to have a restful or peaceful quality, while warmer colours create a more vigorous and assertive mood and darker, more subdued hues can produce a sombre or even sinister atmosphere.

Seeing

I had been travelling through this valley on a midwinter's afternoon when the sky had been filled with dense cloud. But as I neared this location some gaps had developed, allowing small pools of sunlight to play on the landscape, like a travelling spot-light.

Thinking

I wanted to find a viewpoint which would allow me to include some foreground interest and this grey dry-stone wall seemed ideal as it created a bold contrast with the red bracken beyond.

Acting

I set up my camera at this spot and framed the shot so that the curving wall filled the foreground and then waited for the sunlight to reach the area I was aimed at. The sun was very low and, when fully out, cast my own shadow on to the wall, so I had to wait until the foreground was partially in shadow before making my exposures. This has also helped to increase the impact and mood of the shot.

Farndale in the North York Moors, UK

▲ Technical Details
6 x 4.5cm SLR camera with a 55–110mm zoom lens, 81B warm-up and polarising filters on Fuji Velvia.

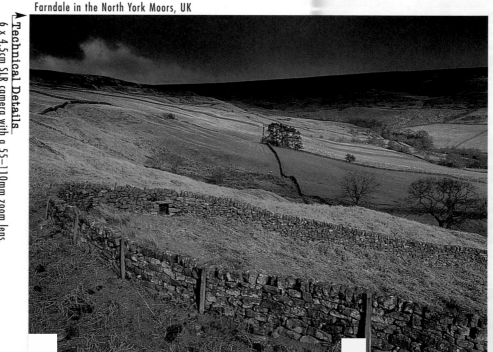

Technical Details

6 x 4.5cm SLR camera with a 55–110mm zoom lens, 81C warm-up and polarising filters on Fuji Velvia.

Dovedale in Derbyshire, UK

The sunlight on this beautiful spring morning created a sparkling quality as it filtered through the trees and, combined with the intense green, monochromatic nature of the scene, produced an image with an upbeat but peaceful atmosphere. I used a polarising filter to increase the colour saturation and the strength of the reflections and a warm-up filter to make the greens even richer.

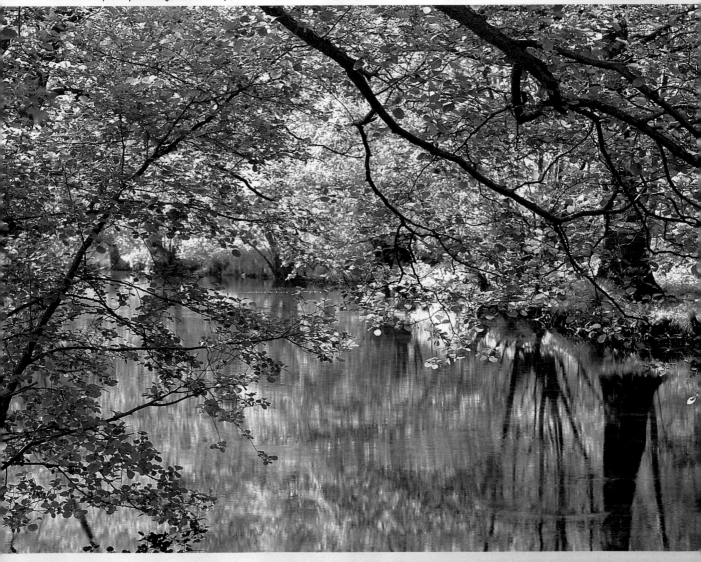

Seeing

It was a slightly misty morning as I travelled through this forest and I had been looking for an interesting arrangement of trees when this very sudden shaft of sunlight appeared.

Thinking

I had only a very short time to set up, frame and shoot the picture as the sun very quickly cleared the mist and soon the shafts of light were no longer visible.

Acting

I had no time to look for different viewpoints and my main concern was to frame the image in a way that created a sense of order in a fairly complex scene while at the same time incorporating the most interesting and dominant shafts of light. I only had time to make a small bracket of exposures and the best frame was one which was slightly darker than normal.

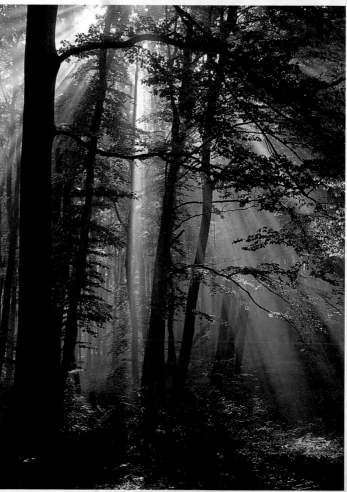

Near Macôn in the Burgundy region of France

Technical Details ➤
6 x 4.5cm SLR camera with a 55–110mm zoom lens and 81B warm-up filter on Fuji Velvia.

Near Condom in the Gascony region of France

This photograph was taken in the afternoon of a hazy summer's day and I was attracted by the pleasing mixture of light and shade together with the fact that the strong highlight on the track was balanced by the small patch of sunlit field visible through the trees towards the right of the frame. I used a long-focus lens to frame a small section of the scene.

Technical Details
35mm SLR camera with a 75–300mm zoom lens, 81C warm-up and polarising filters on Fuji Velvia.

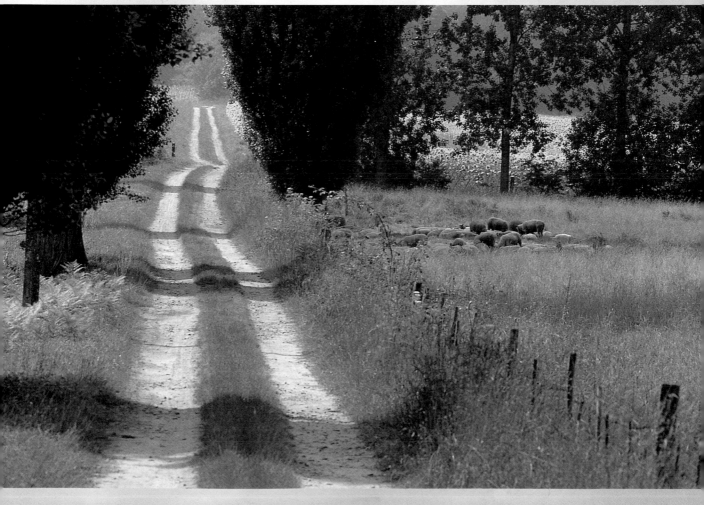

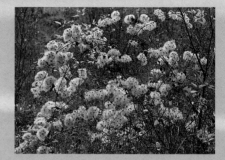

Light & the Garden

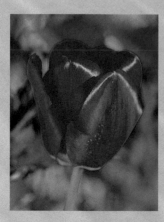

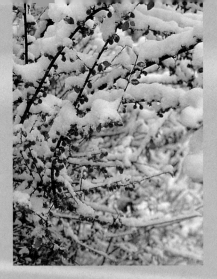

5

The quality and direction of light in a garedenare the two most important factors in creating the mood of an image. From shooting in sunlight to dealing with overcast days, bad weather and the changing seasons, this chapter shows you how to make the best of every situation.

Although most people would choose a sunny day to visit a garden, bright sunlight can produce unattractive effects if some care is not taken over the choice of viewpoint and the way the image is framed. This can be especially true of very bright summer days when the sky is a deep blue and there are no clouds to soften it or to reflect light into the shadows.

Seeing

It was partly the **shadows** created by the sunlight which attracted Julien Busselle to this scene as they **emphasised** the **receding** pathway and heightened the feeling of **depth** which this creates.

Thinking

The trees helped to **accentuate** the receding perspective, and Julien took up a position in the centre of the pathway where the effect was most **noticeable.**

Technical Details
▼ 6 x 4.5cm SLR camera with a 105–210mm zoom lens and an 81B warm-up filter on Fuji Velvia.

Squerryes Court, Westerham in Kent, UK

The striking effect in the photograph of this sambuccus by Julien Busselle is the result of shooting into the light and by the very limited colour range of the image. By choosing the right viewpoint Julien was able to place the back-lit foliage against a virtually black, shadowed background, creating an almost luminous quality.

Acting

Julien framed the image as an upright and used a wide-angle lens to include the closest branch of the nearest tree, providing a frame which helps to direct the interest to the main area of the image and has masked the rather weak sky.

Technical Details

▼ 6 x 4.5cm SLR camera with a 55–110mm zoom lens on Fuji Velvia.

Penshurst Place gardens near Tonbridge in Kent, UK

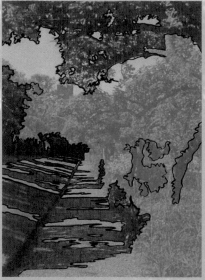

See how the shadows have helped to create the impression of perspective and emphasised the structure of this image.

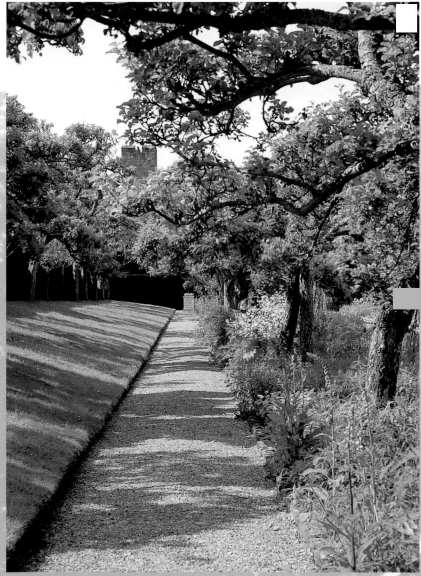

Controlling Contrast

The right level of contrast is very important in colour photography. Too little and the image will appear flat and lacking in colour saturation, too much, and the photograph will be harsh and unappealing, and the subtlety of the colours will be lost.

Seeing

This colourful display of rhododendrons in a woodland garden made an **obvious subject** for a photograph, but the **direct sunlight** of a bright spring day was very hard and there were **dense shadows** which raised the level of contrast to an unacceptable degree.

Thinking

I looked for a **viewpoint** from where the shadows would occupy the **smallest area** and which also placed the most **colourful blooms** together effectively.

Acting

I used my long-focus lens to frame the image **very tightly**, concentrating on the section of the scene where the subject consisted mainly of the **lighter tones**. I used a polarising filter to increase the **colour saturation** and to subdue the highlights, which reduced the contrast further.

Technical Details
▼ 35mm SLR camera with an 80–200mm zoom lens, polarising and 81C warm-up filters on Fuji Velvia.

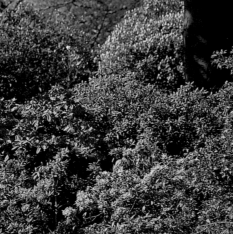

Garden in Kent, UK

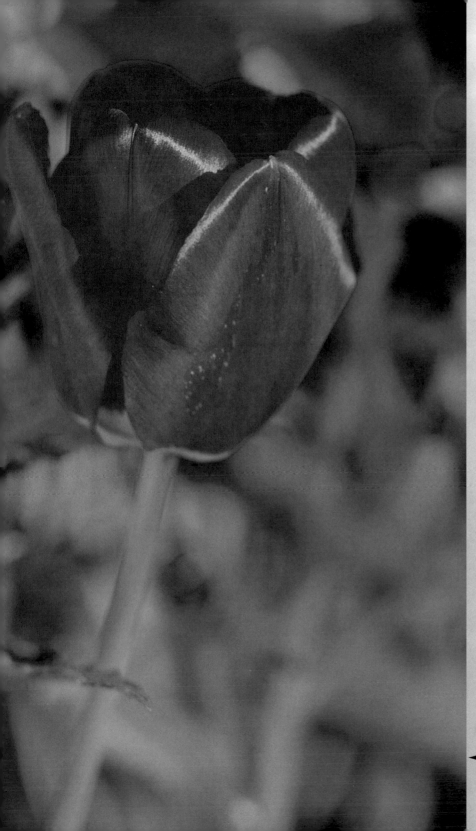

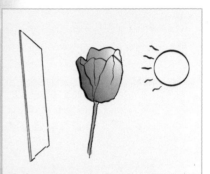

See how the reflector card was placed to reduce the density of the shadows.

Close-up shot of a tulip.

Direct sunlight had created a considerable amount of contrast on this close-up of a tulip and the quality of its colour was greatly diminished because of the dense shadows it created. I used a piece of white card placed very close to the bloom on the shaded side to bounce light back into the shadows, which has almost eliminated them.

Technique

It can help you judge the contrast of a scene if you view it through half-closed eyes or through the viewfinder of an SLR camera with the lens stopped down.

Although the subject, together with the angle and quality of light, is largely responsible for establishing the contrast of an image, considerable control can be achieved by the choice of viewpoint and the way in which the image is framed.

◄ Technical Details
6 x 4.5cm SLR camera with a 105–210mm zoom lens and an extension tube on Fuji Velvia.

Shooting on Cloudy Days

Although a hazy or overcast day may seem less than ideal for photography, it can be preferable for many subjects. Very brightly coloured subjects or those with lots of fine detail will often photograph more successfully when lit by the softer light of a cloudy day. Close-up photographs, in particular, often benefit from being photographed with a more diffused light.

Seeing

My visit to these gardens was on a very overcast day which in some ways restricted my choice of subjects. Although the lighting was ideal for fairly close-up images, I was also keen to produce photographs which showed more of the gardens' character and landscape.

Thinking

I felt that by careful selection and tight framing I could find sections of the garden where the inherent contrast of the scene would make up for the soft lighting and produce images with some impact.

Acting

I found this viewpoint from where, with the aid of a long-focus lens, I was able to isolate a small area of the garden where the colourful flowers and light-toned statues provided enough contrast to create a punchy image.

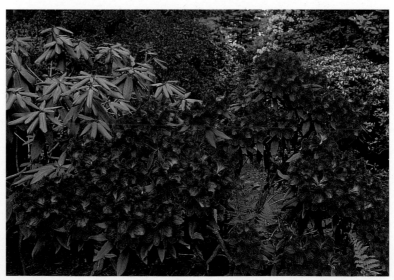

Close-up shot of rhododendrons

The very soft light of an overcast day was the perfect illumination for this close-up shot of rhododendrons. I framed the shot tightly to exclude all but the colour of the blooms and a small area of leaf for contrast and took care to make sure that the featureless, white sky was excluded. I used a small aperture to ensure there was adequate depth of field.

Technical Details
▼ 35mm SLR camera with a 75-300mm zoom lens
and an 81C warm-up filter on Fuji Velvia.

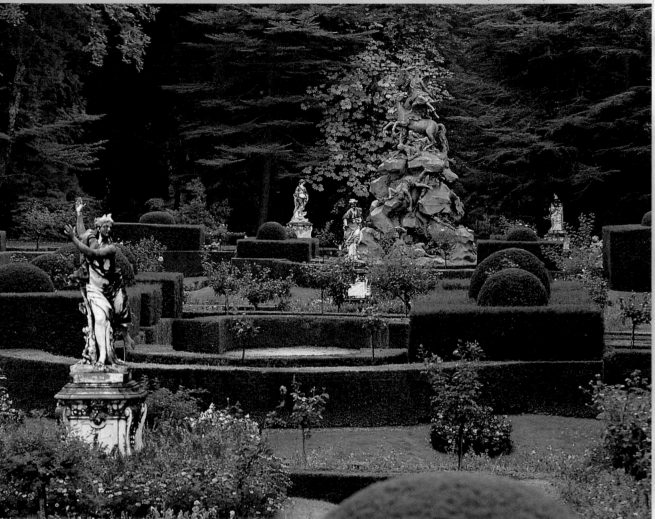

The gardens of San Idelfonso la Granja near Segovia in Castile, Spain

◄**Technical Details**
6 x 4.5cm SLR camera with a
55–110mm zoom lens on Fuji Velvia.

Rule of Thumb

Hazy and overcast days usually have very pale milky
skies, and these can have a very negative effect on
colour photographs when shooting views or distant
scenes. It is best if you can find viewpoints and frame
your pictures to exclude the sky. It can also sometimes
help, especially if there is some tone in the sky, to use a
neutral-graduated filter to make it darker.

The Time of Day

The time of day can have a considerable effect on the quality and mood of a photograph. In the middle of the day the sun reaches its highest peak and the shadows are at their smallest. The colour quality of the light at this time is also at its bluest. Earlier and later in the day the light has a much warmer quality and the shadows lengthen. Also, of course, during the passage of the day the angle of the sun in relation to a particular view changes by almost 180 degrees in high summer.

Technical Details
6 x 4.5cm SLR camera with a 55–110mm zoom lens and an 81B warm-up filter on Fuji Velvia.

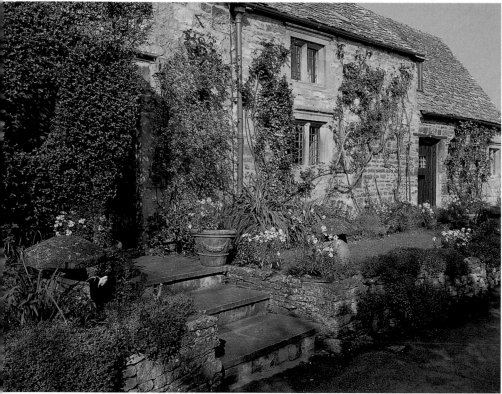

A cottage in the Cotswolds, UK

I'd seen this Cotswold cottage on the previous day when the light had been at a different angle and the front was in deep shade. I made a point of returning the next morning as soon as the sun came up and found the lighting was now ideal.

Rule of Thumb

The warm light at the beginning and end of the day can be particularly effective for photographing buildings and features like walls and ornaments because the lower colour temperature of this light brings out the rich colour and texture of old stone.

Technical Details
▼ 35mm SLR camera with an 80–200mm zoom lens, polarising and 81C warm-up filters on Fuji Velvia.

The warm light of the sun at the very end of the day has accentuated the rich colour of the autumn foliage in this shot, as well as helping to create an atmospheric image.

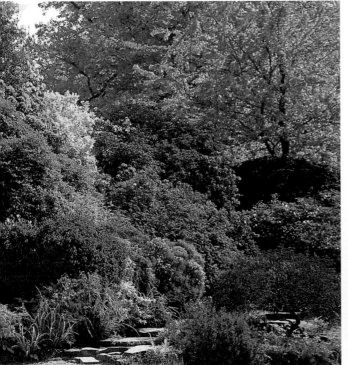

The gardens of Hever Castle near Edenbridge in Kent, UK

During the first part of my visit to this garden, in the early morning, the lighting on this magnificent display of Rhododendrons had been unattractive as it had cast some quite deep shadows within the banks of foliage and bloom, and had created considerable contrast. But when I returned a few hours later the sun was higher in the sky and the shadows had become much smaller and were no longer too dominant.

Technical Details ►
6 x 4.5cm SLR camera with a 105–210mm zoom lens and a 81B warm-up filter on Fuji Velvia.

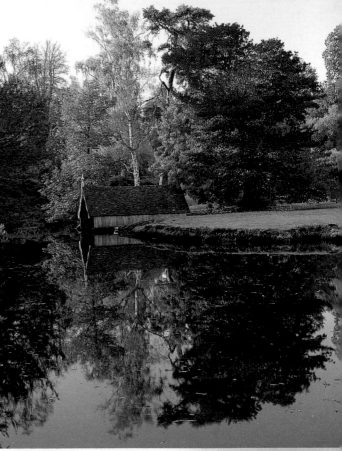

The gardens of Scotney Castle near Tunbridge Wells in Kent, UK

Light & Colour

The colour quality of daylight varies considerably according to the position of the sun in the sky and factors like cloud and blue sky. In the middle of a summer's day, when there is a deep blue sky, the light can be much bluer than that for which the film is balanced. Likewise, shooting subjects in open shade and on a cloudy overcast day can create an unpleasant blue cast on transparency film. On the other hand, early morning and late afternoon sunlight can be much yellower than that for which the film is balanced and this can create a warm colour cast.

Seeing

The back lighting created a very attractive quality in this autumnal scene. It was quite early in the morning and the sunlight had a warmth which accentuated the colour of the red leaves and golden grasses.

Thinking

I realised that the deeply shaded background had a quite pronounced blue cast because of light reflected from the blue sky and felt that this provided an effective contrast with the warm foreground colours.

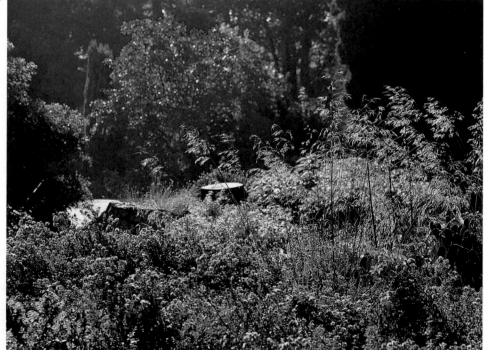

Technical Details ▸
6 x 4.5cm SLR camera with a 105–210mm zoom lens on Fuji Velvia.

Garden in Kent, UK

Acting

I decided to use a long-focus lens to isolate the most colourful area of the foreground and chose a viewpoint which placed it in the most effective juxtaposition to the shadowed background.

Nymans garden, near Haywards Heath in West
Sussex, UK.

This photograph was taken in late afternoon
when the colour quality of the light was very
warm. This has accentuated the rich red tones
of the autumn foliage.

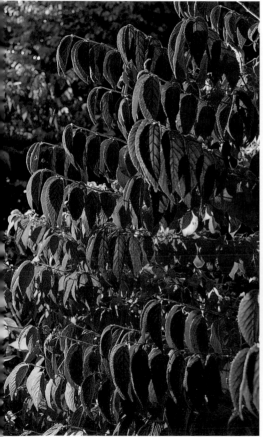

Technical Details
6 x 4.5cm SLR camera with a 105–210mm
zoom lens, polarising and 81A warm-up filters
on Fuji Velvia.

Technical Details
6 x 4.5cm SLR camera with a 105–210mm zoom lens and an 81C warm-up filter on Fuji Velvia.

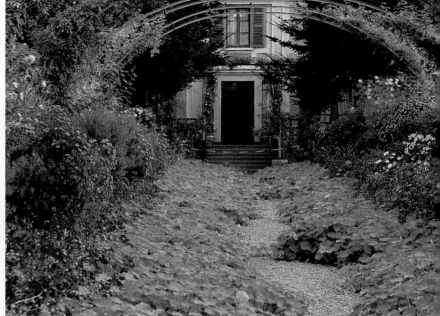

Monet's Garden at Giverny near Vernon in Normandy, France

This shot was taken on a very overcast day when the colour
temperature of the light was quite high. This would have created
a distinctly blue cast so I used an 81C warm-up filter to
counteract this and framed the image quite tightly to fill the
frame with the greatest concentration of colour and to eliminate
the featureless white sky.

Seeing

This photograph was taken in the open shade on a sunny day with a blue sky and the colour quality of the light was quite blue.

Thinking

It was the contrast between the vivid autumnal colours of the boston ivy and green leaves of the hydrangeas which appealed to me and I thought that this might be diminished if I used a warm-up filter.

Rule of Thumb

When photographing close-up images of flowers which have very warm colours, such as oranges, reds and yellows, it's often best either not to use warm-up filters at all, or to use only very weak ones, even on overcast days or in open shade, as the effect can be too strong.

Technical Details

▼ 6 x 4.5cm SLR camera with a 55–110mm zoom lens on Fuji Velvia.

Hedgerow in Burgundy, France

I found this clump of forget-me-nots in a hedgerow while driving through the countryside in Burgundy in France. on a cloudy day. It was the overall bluishness of the subject which appealed to me and, although I could have used a warm-up filter to correct this, I felt the image would benefit from having a cool, blue quality.

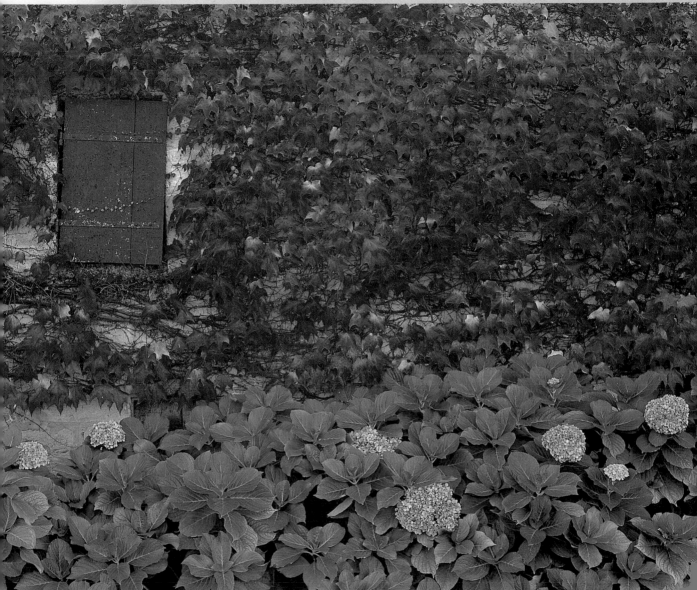

Acting

I decided to shoot the picture **without a filter** but to frame the image very tightly so that the picture was almost filled by the green and red leaves. The resulting **blue cast** has had little significant effect on the red leaves but has given the green leaves a distinctly bluish quality which, I think, **increases the contrast** between them.

The Weather

A warm, sunny summer's day is the sort of occasion upon which most photographers would think of heading off to shoot pictures of a garden. But weather conditions such as fog, frost and stormy skies can give an image an instantly eye-catching quality and create a degree of interest and impact which can be lacking in the more bland light of a perfect sunny day.

Seeing

This woodland garden had been transformed by the fog in this picture taken by Julien Busselle. On a previous visit he had shot pictures in sunlight which were very pleasing but on this occasion there was far more atmosphere.

Thinking

Julien decided to make a skimmia bush the main feature of this shot because the bold colour provides an essential element of contrast together with the dark tree trunk on the right-hand side of the frame.

Acting

He used a long-focus lens to isolate a small area of the scene and chose a viewpoint which included the more distant semi-silhouetted trees, framing the image quite tightly to emphasise the strong colours and shapes.

Rule of Thumb

Bad weather conditions like fog and overcast skies often result in a lack of contrast. To overcome this you can choose viewpoints and frame your pictures in such a way that the darkest tones and richest colours are placed quite close to the camera. Brightly coloured flowers, for instance, or the silhouetted branches of a tree in the foreground, can considerably increase the contrast of an image.

Technical Details
35mm SLR camera with a 75–300mm zoom lens and a 81B warm-up filter on Fuji Velvia.

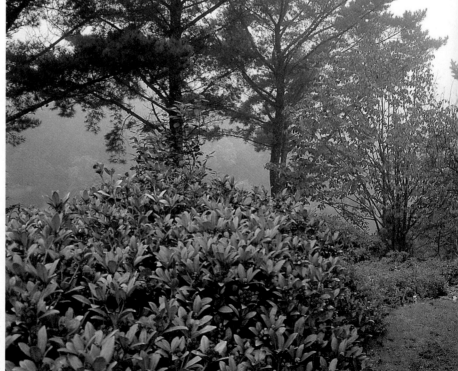

Marwood Hill near Barnstaple in North Devon, UK

Near Chateau Meillant
in the department of
Cher, France

This shot of a summer
meadow filled with wild
flowers was taken very
shortly after a storm
had cleared, and the
combination of the
sunlit foreground
flowers and the dark
stormy sky above has
given the image
considerable impact. I
used a wide-angle lens
to allow the inclusion of
close foreground details
and a neutral-
graduated filter to
emphasise the dark sky.

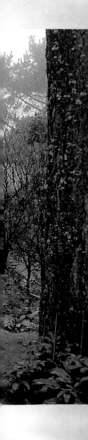

▲ Technical Details
35mm SLR camera with a 20–35mm zoom lens, 81B warm-up and neutral-graduated filters on Fuji Velvia.

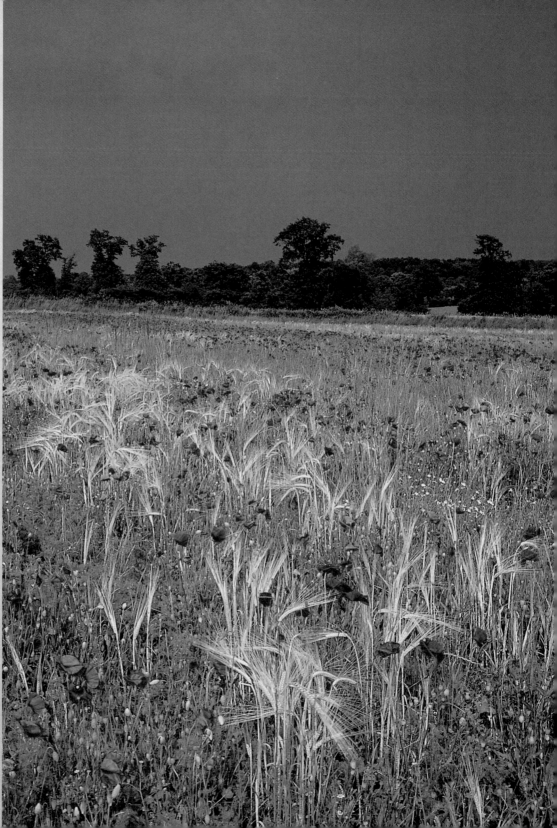

One of the most appealing aspects of garden photography is the constant changes which take place as the year progresses. The effects of the seasons are, of course, visible generally in the countryside but gardens are designed and planted with these changes in mind. It's possible to visit the same garden at intervals throughout the year and find it very different on each occasion.

A Year in a Garden

Photographing a garden year can be a very satisfying way of building a collection of photographs, whether it is on visits to the same garden or by choosing gardens which reach their peaks at particular times of the year.

Seeing

I saw this small Sussex cottage garden as I walked along the street and was immediately struck by the beautiful summery quality of its colour and of the light.

Thinking

I wanted to capture the smallness and intimacy of the space and decided to make use of the wrought-iron gate in the foreground.

Acting

I chose a viewpoint which allowed me to include part of the gate with a wide-angle lens and to frame the shot so that just the top was visible along with the roses on the left-hand side of the picture.

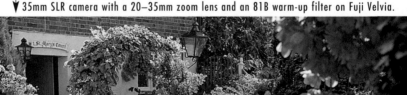

Technical Details
▼ 35mm SLR camera with a 20–35mm zoom lens and an 81B warm-up filter on Fuji Velvia.

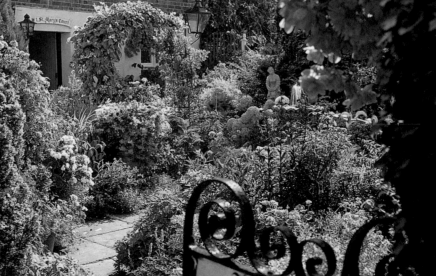

Cottage garden in Sussex, UK

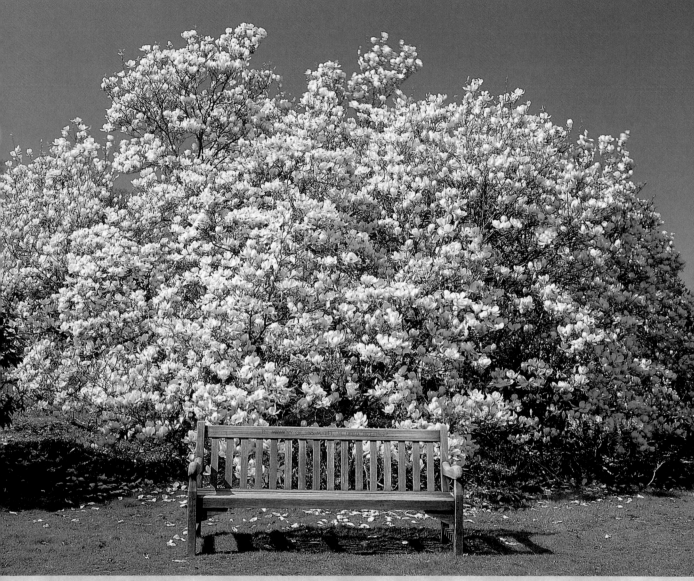

Technical Details

6 x 4.5cm SLR camera with a 55–110mm zoom lens, polarising and 81C warm-up filters on Fuji Velvia.

Rule of Thumb

When shooting subjects which have a large area of very light tones, like this shot of the magnolia tree, it's necessary to increase your exposure because a normal exposure reading will interpret the scene as being brighter than it really is and indicate less exposure than is actually needed.

Emmett's Gardens near Sevenoaks in Kent, UK

I decided to adopt a very straightforward approach to photographing this magnificent magnolia tree. I was lucky because the sunlight was at the perfect angle from this viewpoint, giving me a front-on view of the tree with the bench in the centre. The cloudless blue sky above was a bonus because it kept the image very simple. I used a polarising filter to increase the colour saturation of the sky and create stronger relief with the blooms. I gave two-thirds of a stop extra exposure to allow for the large area of very bright flowers.

Seeing

I was driving through a small valley in the French Pyrenees when I saw this prunus orchard in late autumn. Although it was a cloudy, overcast day, the soft light had made the rich gold of the leaves appear almost luminous.

Thinking

I felt that the most striking effect would be achieved by filling the frame with the colour of the foliage and looked for a section of the orchard where this was densest.

Acting

I chose this viewpoint because the shapes created by the branches and trunks of the trees created a very pleasing arrangement, and I liked the small intrusion of green grass on the left-hand side of the shot. I used my zoom lens to frame the image quite precisely, excluding the white, featureless sky above the tree tops.

Prunus orchard in the Pyrenees, France

▲ Technical Details
6 x 4.5cm SLR camera with a 105–210mm zoom lens and an 81B warm-up filter on Fuji Velvia.

▲ Technical Details
6 x 4.5cm SLR camera with a 105–210mm zoom lens and an 81B warm-up filter on Fuji Velvia.

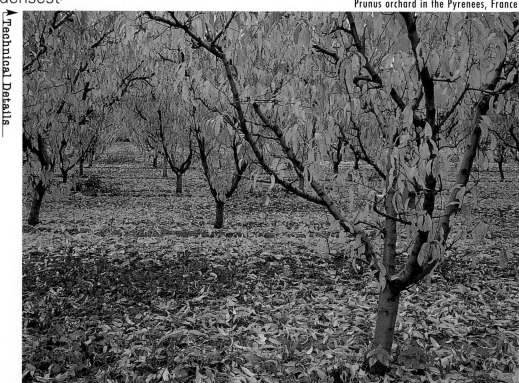

The North Downs in Kent, UK

Great drifts of old man's beard cover the North Downs near my home in Kent in the early winter, and I couldn't resist taking this shot. There was a very soft hazy sunlight and I took this picture towards the light using a viewpoint which placed the red and gold autumnal foliage behind to create a contrasting background. I used a long-focus lens to frame a small section of the bush and chose a fairly wide aperture so the background details were slightly out of focus and not too distracting.

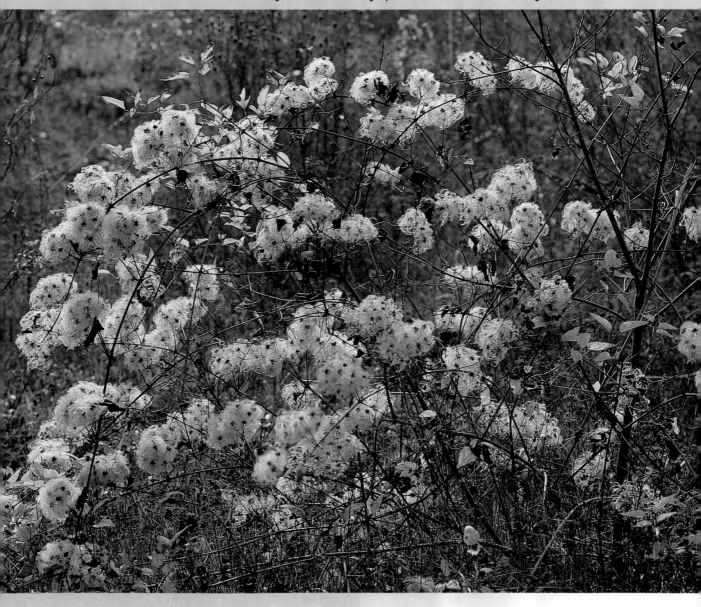

The Seasons

Garden in Kent, UK

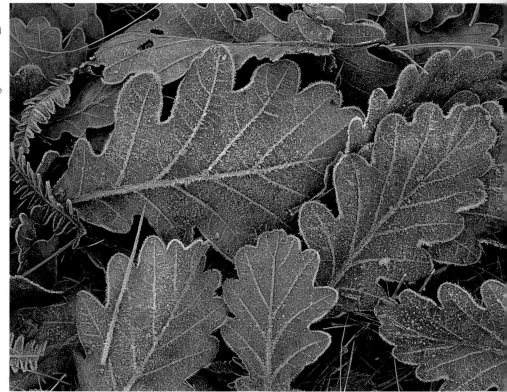

Seeing

A hoar frost had blanketed this woodland garden when I visited it early on a winter morning. I discovered this group of leaves which were in good condition and nicely arranged – the frost made it impossible to do any rearranging without marking it.

Thinking

I wanted to shoot a close-up image so that the texture of the frost would be visible, and as this would give me a very limited depth of field, I opted to use an overhead viewpoint so that the leaves were on a parallel plane to the camera.

Acting

I moved my tripod and adjusted the zoom until I had the group of leaves arranged within the frame to my liking. The sun was just beginning to rise enough to reach the leaves and I waited until they were just tinged with sunlight before shooting.

Garden in Kent, UK

A heavy fall of snow can seriously limit the possibilities of garden photography, but the red berries of this cotoneaster peeping through the snow-covered branches were just prominent enough to make the image work. I framed the picture tightly, isolating the most concentrated area of berries, and gave a half stop extra exposure to compensate for the bright snow.

Technical Details

6 x 4.5cm SLR camera with a 105–210mm zoom lens and extension tube on Fuji Velvia.

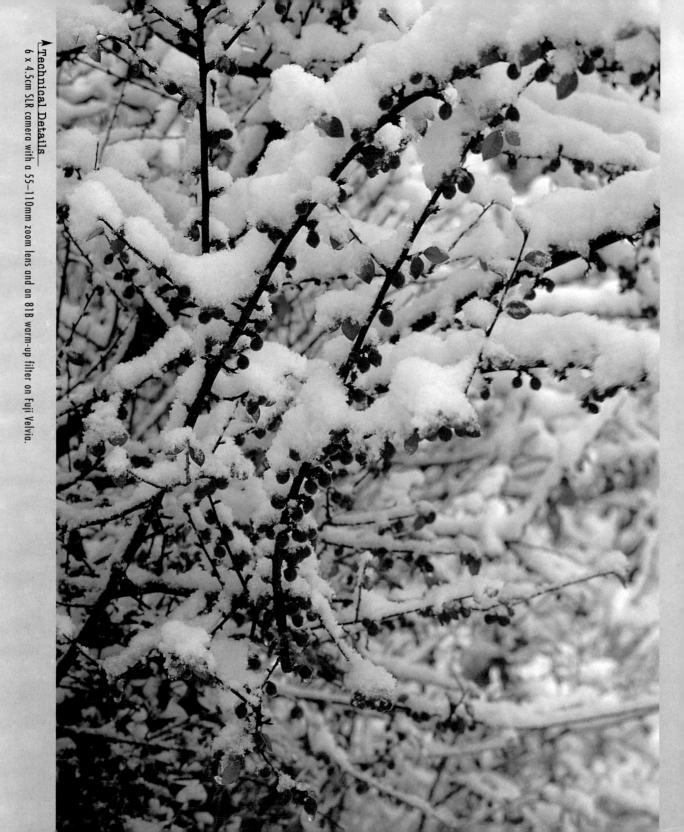

▲ Technical Details
6 x 4.5cm SLR camera with a 55–110mm zoom lens and an 81B warm-up filter on Fuji Velvia.

Cameras & Equipment

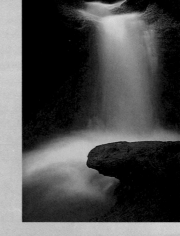

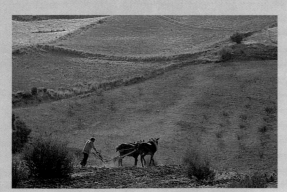

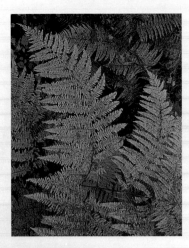

6

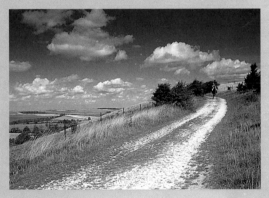

The choice of equipment for landscape and garden photography is an entirely personal one as even the simplest camera is capable, in the right hands, of producing striking images. In this chapter the advantages and benefits of different systems are described to help determine the best choice for your particular interests.

The choice of camera type and format for landscape & garden photography depends upon a number of factors. Versatility is one of the most important, since landscapes and gardens can involve such widely varying subjects as buildings, still lives, details and close-ups.

Formats

Image size is the most basic consideration. The image area of a 35mm camera is approximately 24 x 36mm but with roll-film it can be from 45 x 60mm up to 90 x 60mm according to camera choice. The degree of enlargement needed to provide, say, an A4 reproduction is considerably less for a roll-film format than for 35mm and gives a potentially higher image quality.

For most photographers the choice is between 35mm and 120 roll-film cameras. Advanced Photo System (APS) cameras offer a format slightly smaller than 35mm while for images larger than 90 x 60mm it is necessary to use a view camera using sheet film of 5 x 4in or 10 x 8in format.

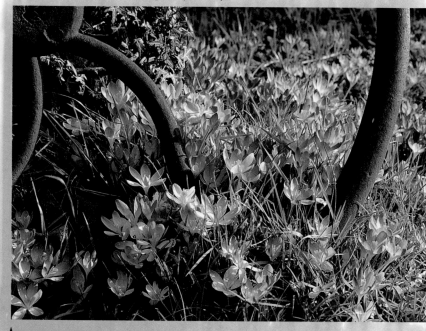

Autumn crocuses
in Kent, UK

This shot of autumn crocuses benefits from the use of a medium-format camera with the greater image quality which roll-film transparencies and negatives can offer. This format is ideal for those wishing to see their work in print, for high-quality projection and for producing large prints.

Technical Details
6 x 4.5cm SLR camera with a 105–210mm zoom lens on Fuji Velvia.

Pros & Cons

APS cameras have a more limited choice of film types and accessories and are designed primarily for the use of print film. 35mm **Single Lens Reflex** (SLR) cameras are provided with the **widest range** of film types and accessories and provide the best compromise between image quality, size, weight and cost of equipment.

Both **accessories and film** are significantly more expensive with **roll-film cameras** and the range of lenses and accessories is more limited than with 35mm equipment. Some facilities, such as autofocus and motor drive, are not available on many roll-film cameras, and these cameras are also generally **heavier and bulkier** than 35mm cameras. View cameras provide extensive perspective and depth-of-field control and are especially useful for architectural and still-life photography but are cumbersome and not user friendly.

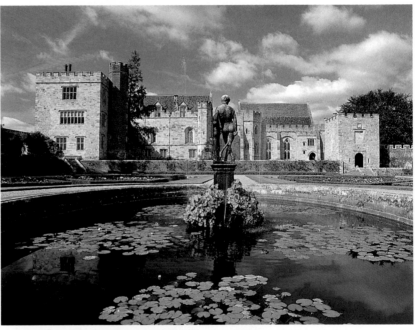

Penshurst Place near Tonbridge in Kent, UK

A shot like this, taken using a very wide-angle lens, requires a camera with interchangeable lenses. These can be significantly less expensive for 35mm cameras than for medium-format ones.

The village of Vieux Port near Rouen in Normandy, France.

A fairly simple APS or 35mm compact camera is ideal for shots like this taken in good light, when colour negative film is used and prints of no larger than about 10 x 8in are required.

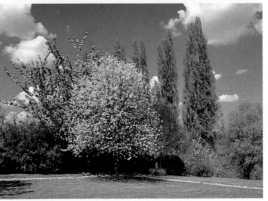

▲ Technical Details
35mm compact camera with a 35–70mm zoom lens on Fuji Super G 200.

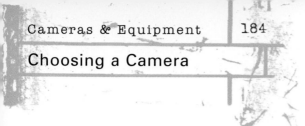

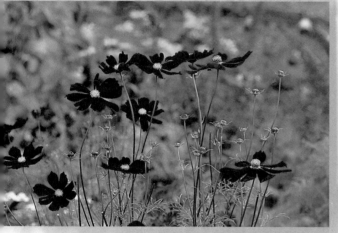

Annual cosmos, UK countryside

An SLR camera is ideal for shots like this close-up
of the annual cosmos because the effect of
focusing can be seen clearly whereas a viewfinder
camera shows the entire image as sharp
regardless of where it is focused. An SLR camera
with a depth of field preview button will make it
easier to judge the effect of focusing when using
different apertures.

↑ Technical Details
35mm SLR camera with an 80–200mm
zoom lens on Fuji Velvia.

Camera Types

There are two basic choices for both roll-film and 35mm
cameras: the viewfinder (rangefinder) camera and the
Single Lens Reflex (SLR).

Pros & Cons

An SLR camera allows you to view the actual
image which is being recorded on the film while
a viewfinder camera uses a separate
optical system. The effect of focusing can
be seen on the screen of an SLR but the whole image
appears in focus when seen through a viewfinder
camera.

Generally, facilities like autofocus and
exposure control are more accurate and
convenient with SLR cameras and with them you can
see the effect of filters and attachments – which you
can't do with a viewfinder. SLR cameras have a much
wider range of accessories and
lenses available and are more suited to subjects
like wildlife which demand very long-focus lenses and
close-ups. However, viewfinder cameras tend to be
lighter and quieter than SLRs.

A bluebell wood near Ashford in Kent, UK

The elongated format of a panoramic camera
does not suit every subject, especially when
using the more extreme 6 x 17cm format, but
it can be very effective.

Technical Details →
A 5 x 4in viewfinder camera fitted with a 6 x
12cm roll-film back; 90mm lens on Fuji Velvia.

Specialist Cameras

While it's possible to produce panoramic format photographs with some ordinary APS cameras, 35mm and roll-film cameras, dedicated 6 x 12cm, 6 x 17cm and 6 x 24cm cameras are the professional's choice, particularly for garden landscapes. These are essentially viewfinder cameras taking 120 roll-film with a greatly elongated film chamber. Some have fixed wide-angle lenses while others have interchangeable lenses. An alternative to using a dedicated panoramic camera is to use a 6 x 12cm roll-film back with a 5 x 4in view camera.

In addition to conventional panoramic cameras there are also swing-lens cameras, such as the Widelux, giving a panoramic image over a wide angle of view. These can be bought in both 35mm and 120 film formats and have a moving lens mount which progressively exposes the film. This gives a more limited range of shutter speeds and also causes horizontal lines to curve if the camera is not held completely level.

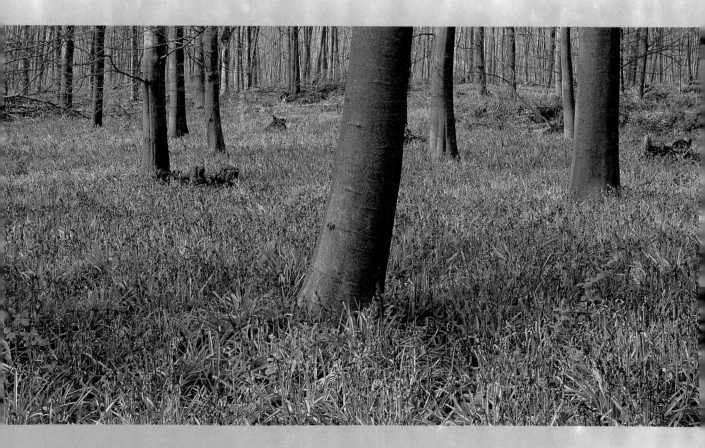

A **standard lens** is one which creates a field of view of about 45% degrees, approximating that of normal vision, and has a focal length equivalent to the diagonal measurement of the film format i.e. 50mm with a 35mm camera and 80mm with a 6 x 6cm camera.

Lenses with a **shorter focal length** create a **wider field of view** and those with a longer focal length produce a narrower field of view.

Zoom lenses provide a wide range of focal lengths within a single optic, taking up less space and offering more convenience than having several fixed-focal-length lenses.

Pros & Cons

Many inexpensive zooms have a maximum aperture of f5.6 or smaller. This can be quite restricting when fast shutter speeds are needed in low-light levels and a fixed-focal-length lens with a wider maximum aperture of f2.8 or f4 can sometimes be a better choice.

Zoom lenses are available for most 35mm SLR cameras over a wide range of focal lengths but it's important to appreciate that the image quality will drop with lenses which are designed to cover more than about a three to one ratio, i.e. 28-85mm or 70-210mm.

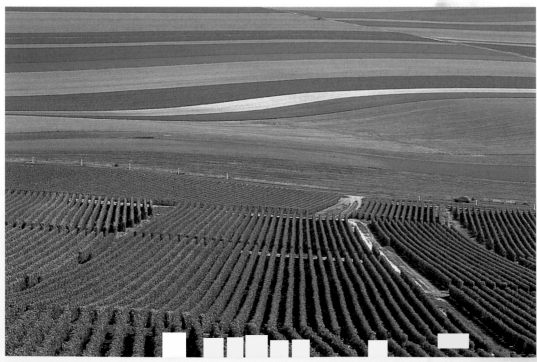

Mont Aimee near Bergeres-les-Vertus in the Champagne region of France

A long-focus lens enables you to isolate a small area of a scene from a distant viewpoint and is invaluable for emphasising elements like pattern and texture in a landscape image.

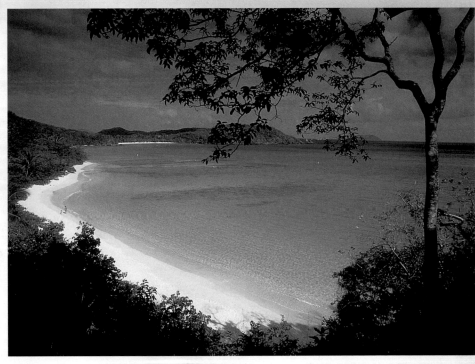

Hawk's Nest Bay in St John, US Virgin Island

I used a wide-angle lens to enable me to use the tree in the close foreground as a frame for the distant scene, which has helped to create a sense of depth and distance in the image.

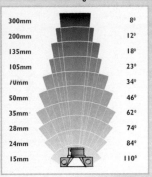

300mm	8°
200mm	12°
135mm	18°
105mm	23°
70mm	34°
50mm	46°
35mm	62°
28mm	74°
24mm	84°
15mm	110°

This illustration shows the comparative fields of view given with lenses of varying focal lengths when used with a 35mm camera.

Special Lenses

A perspective-control or shift lens can sometimes be useful for landscape photography, especially if buildings are occasionally included. These allow the lens to be physically moved from its axis to enable the image to be moved higher or lower in the frame without the need to tilt the camera, thereby avoiding converging verticals. In this way, the camera's field of view can be lowered to include foreground details, for example, or raised to include more of the sky without the accompanying distortion.

A macro lens is very useful when photographing close-up images of natural forms, making it possible to obtain up to life-sized images without the need for extension tubes or close-up attachments.

Extenders can allow you to increase the focal length of an existing lens – a x1.4 extender will turn a 200mm lens into a 280mm and a x2 extender will make it 400mm. There will be some loss of sharpness with all but the most expensive optics and a reduction in maximum aperture of one and two stops respectively.

Technical Details
35mm SLR camera with a 20–35mm zoom lens, 81C warm-up and polarising filters on Fuji Velvia.

Technical Details
35mm SLR camera with a 75–300mm zoom lens, 81B warm-up and polarising filters on Fuji Velvia.

There is a wide range of accessories which can be used to control the quality of the image and increase the camera's capability. Extension tubes, bellows units and dioptre lenses will all allow the lens to be focused at a closer distance than it's designed for. This can be useful for obvious close-up subjects like flowers.

Technical Details
6 x 4.5cm SLR camera with a 105–210mm zoom lens, an extension tube on Fuji Velvia.

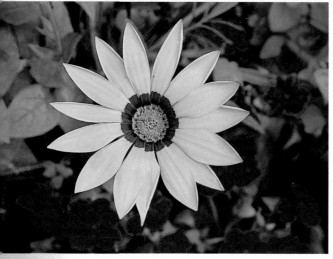

Close-up of a gazania bloom

Filters

A range of filters is essential for both colour and black-and-white photography and a square filter system, such as Cokin or HiTech, is by far the most convenient and practical option. These systems use a universal filter holder which is slipped on to a simple adaptor ring available in all lens-thread diameters. In this way the same filter holder can be fitted to all your lenses.

The most basic filter kit should include a set of warm-up filters, a graduated filter and a polarising filter. For those shooting black-and-white film, a few contrast filters, such as yellow or red, are a useful addition. Polarisers are available in either linear or circular form. The former can interfere with some auto-focusing and exposure systems. Your camera's instruction book should give you more details, but if in doubt, use a circular polariser.

The combination of a zoom lens and extension tubes allows a wide degree of control over both the image size and the distance between camera and subject when shooting close-ups, as in this picture of a gazania bloom.

Powerscourt Gardens near Wicklow in County Wicklow, Eire

Although this photograph was taken in bright light, a tripod was essential as I had to use a slow shutter speed of 1/2 sec. This was the result of using a slow film of ISO 50 in conjunction with a polarising filter and a small aperture of f22 to obtain maximum depth of field.

Technical Details
6 x 4.5cm SLR camera with a 105–210mm zoom lens on Fuji Velvia.

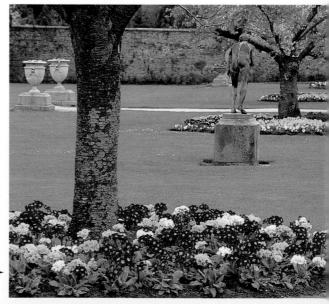

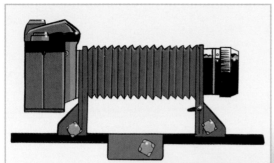

A bellows unit for use with a 35mm SLR camera.

Technical Details

▼ 6 x 4.5cm SLR camera with a 105–210mm zoom lens on Fuji Velvia.

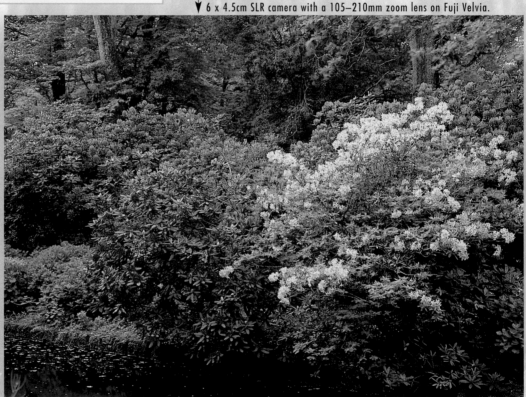

The woodland garden of Chateau Grand Puy Lacoste in the Medoc, France

Although this scene appears quite brightly lit, it was, in fact, a very gloomy, overcast day and the dark, wooded setting, combined with the use of a slow film and a polarising filter, made the necessary exposure of two seconds impossible without a tripod.

Tripod

Perhaps one of the most important accessories is a good solid tripod as it can greatly improve image sharpness allowing you to shoot pictures in low light levels and to use small apertures for greater depth of field. A shake-free means of firing the camera, such as a cable release or a remote trigger, is advisable when using a tripod-mounted camera.

Flash Guns

A separate flash gun is more useful than a built in flash. It will be much more powerful than one built in and it can be used off camera, fitted with a diffuser and used as a fill in to reduce contrast when shooting in bright sunlight.

The **aperture** is the device which controls the brightness of the image falling upon the film and is indicated by f stop numbers: f 2, f2.8, f4, f5.6, f8, f11, f16, f 22 and f32. Each step down, from f2.8 to f4, for example, reduces the amount of light reaching the film by 50% and each step up, from f8 to f5.6, for instance, doubles the brightness of the image.

The **shutter speed** settings control the length of times for which the image is allowed to play on the film and, in conjunction with the aperture, control the exposure and quality of the image. These are provided either in one-stop increments, such as 1/60 second to 1/125 second; half-stop increments, from 1/60 second to 1/100 second; or one-third of a stop increments, from 1/60 second to 1/80 second, for example.

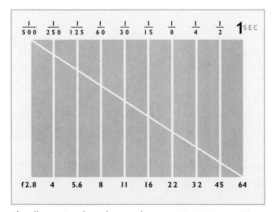

This illustration shows how as the aperture is made smaller and the shutter speed made slower the same amount of exposure is given.

Technique

Choice of aperture also influences the **depth of field**, which is the distance in front and beyond the point at which the lens is focused. At **wide apertures**, like f2.8, the depth of field is quite limited, making closer and more distant details appear distinctly out of focus.

The effect becomes more pronounced as the **focal length** of the lens increases and as the focusing distance decreases. So with, say, a 200mm lens focused at two metres and an aperture of f2.8 the range of sharp focus will extend only a very short distance in front and behind.

The **depth of field increases** when a smaller aperture is used and when using a short focal length, or wide-angle lens. In this way a 24mm lens focused at, say, 50 metres at an aperture of f22 would provide a wide range of sharp focus extending from quite close to the camera to infinity.

A camera with a depth-of-field preview button will allow you to judge the depth of field in the viewfinder. An indication of the depth of field at different apertures is marked on the **focusing mount** of most lenses.

Technical Details

35mm SLR camera with a 35mm lens and an 81B warm-up filter on Fuji Velvia.

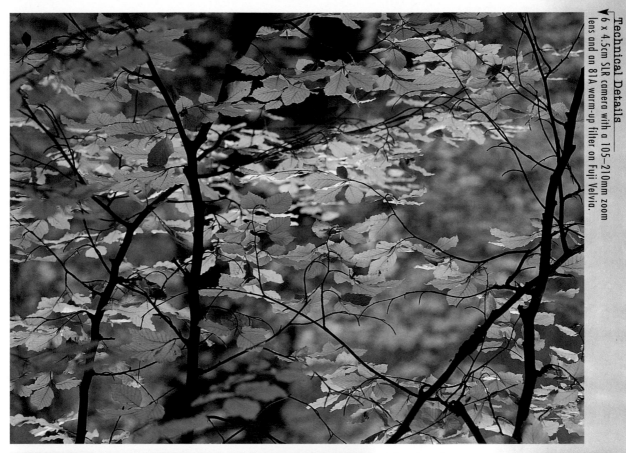

Technical Details
6 x 4.5cm SLR camera with a 105–210mm zoom lens and an 81A warm-up filter on Fuji Velvia.

Fishpond Woods near Sevenoaks in Kent, UK

I used a long-focus lens and selected a wide aperture so that only the closest leaves would be sharp and the more distant details recorded as a soft, out-of-focus blur.

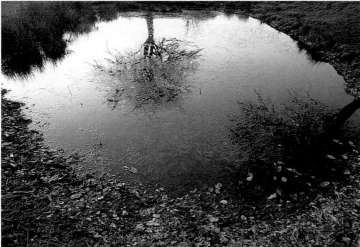

Knole Park near Sevenoaks in Kent, UK

I needed to use a small aperture of f22 to provide enough depth of field to ensure that both the details at the edge of the pond and the reflection of the distant trees were equally sharp.

Apertures & Shutter Speeds

Shutter Speeds

The choice of shutter speed determines the degree of sharpness with which a moving subject will be recorded. With a fast-moving subject like a fountain, a shutter speed of 1/1000 sec or faster will be necessary to obtain a sharp image of the droplets.

In bright light it is not always possible to use very slow shutter speeds and there is an effective alternative method which involves making a number of exposures on the same frame using the camera's multi-exposure facility. If your exposure reading is, say, 1/30 at f16 you can give eight exposures of 1/250 sec at the same aperture or 16 exposures of 1/500 sec. The cumulative exposure will be the same but the moving part of the subject will create a similar effect to a very slow shutter speed.

Technique

A sharp image of a moving subject is not always the best way of photographing it, however, and in some circumstances a very slow shutter speed can be used to create striking effects. A classic example is a waterfall.

A tripod must be used to ensure the static elements of the image are recorded sharply and then a slow shutter speed of, say, one second or more can be selected to create a fluid smoke-like effect.

Rule of Thumb

The choice of shutter speed can also affect the image sharpness of a static subject when the camera is hand-held, as even slight camera shake can easily blur the image. The effect is more pronounced with long-focus lenses and when shooting close-ups. The safest minimum shutter speed should be considered as a reciprocal of the focal length of the lens being used – 1/200 sec with a 200mm lens, for instance.

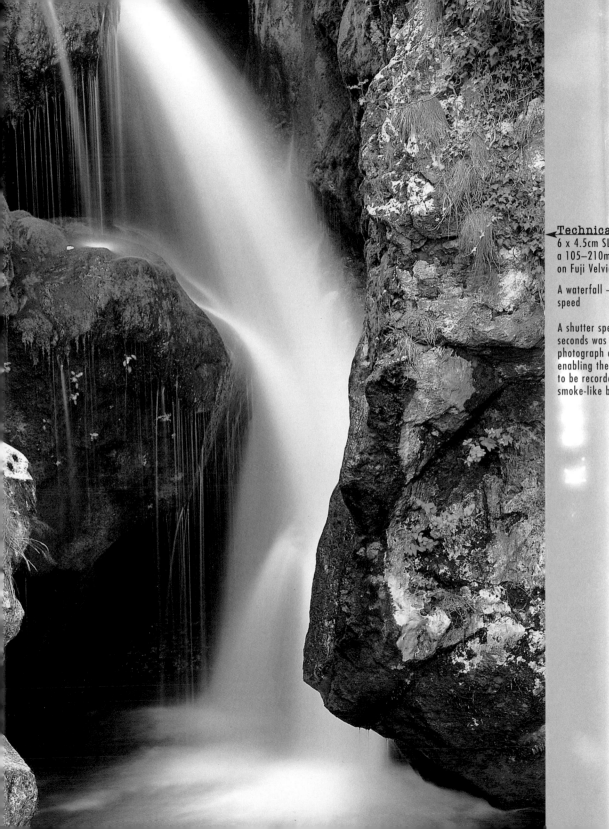

◄Technical Details
6 x 4.5cm SLR camera with
a 105–210mm zoom lens
on Fuji Velvia.

A waterfall – slow shutter
speed

A shutter speed of two
seconds was used for this
photograph of a waterfall,
enabling the moving water
to be recorded as a soft,
smoke-like blur.

Understanding Exposures

Modern cameras with automatic exposure systems have
made some aspects of achieving good-quality images
much easier, but no system is infallible and an understanding of how exposure
meters work will help to ensure a higher success rate.

An exposure meter, whether it's a built-in TTL meter or a separate hand meter, works on the principle that the subject it is aimed at is a mid-tone, know as an 18% grey. In practice, of course, the subject is invariably a mixture of tones and colours but the assumption is still that, if mixed together, like so many pots of different-coloured paints, the resulting blend would still be the same 18% grey tone.

With most subjects the reading taken from the whole of the image will produce a satisfactory exposure. But if there are aspects of a subject which are abnormal – when it contains large areas of very light or dark tones, for example – the reading needs to be modified.

An exposure reading from a snow drift for instance, would, if uncorrected, record it as grey on film. In the same way a reading taken from a very dark subject would result in it being overexposed and appearing too light on the film.

Technical Details
▼ 35mm SLR camera with a 35-70mm zoom lens, 81C
warm-up and polarising filters on Fuji Velvia.

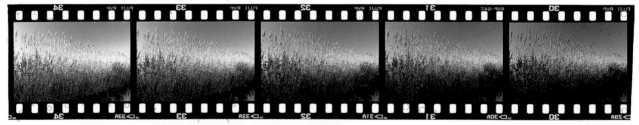

These five exposures were bracketed giving one and two-thirds of a stop
less than the meter indicated and one and two-thirds of a stop more. The
transparencies which have had less exposure show more highlight detail,
less shadow detail and greater colour saturation and those that have had
more exposure have less highlight detail, more shadow detail and less
colour saturation.

The River Ouysse near Rocamadour in the Lot region of France

I gave two-thirds of a stop more exposure than the meter indicated for this photograph as the very bright highlights on the water suggested less exposure than was needed and would have resulted in the image being too dark.

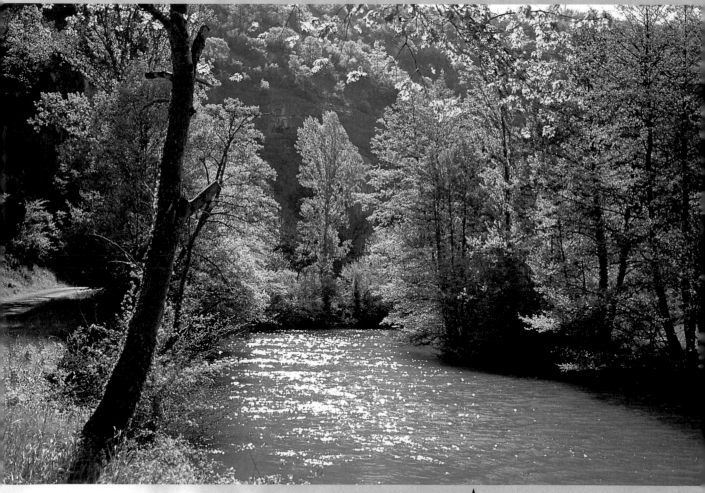

Technical Details ↑

35mm SLR camera with a 35–70mm zoom lens 81C warm-up and polarising filters on Fuji Velvia.

The most common situations in which the **exposure** taken from a normal, average reading needs to be **increased** are when shooting into the **light**, when there are large areas of white or very light tones in the scene, such as a snow scene for example, and when there is a large area of bright sky in the frame.

The exposure needs to be **decreased** when the subject is essentially **dark** in tone or when there are large areas of shadow close to the camera. With abnormal subjects it is often possible to take a close-up or spot reading from an area which is of normal, average tone.

Technique

With **negative films** there is a **latitude** one stop or more each way and small variations in exposure errors will not be important but with transparency film even a slight variation will make a significant difference to the image quality and, where possible, it's best to bracket exposures giving, a third or half a stop more and less than that indicated, even with normal subjects.

Technical Details
6 x 4.5cm SLR camera with a 55–110mm zoom lens on Fuji Velvia. ▼

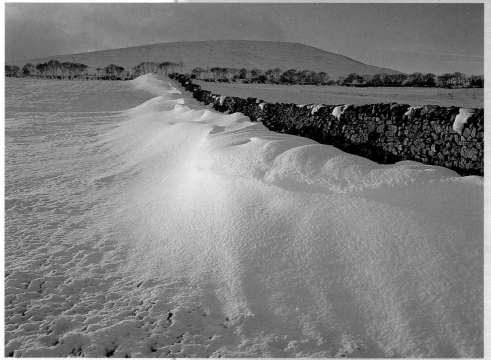

Ribblesdale in Yorkshire, UK

For this sunlit snow scene I needed to give one stop more than the exposure meter indicated to avoid this image recording too darkly.

Rule of Thumb

Many cameras allow you to take a spot reading from a small area of a scene as well as an average reading and this can be useful for calculating the exposure with subjects of an abnormal tonal range or of high contrast. Switching between the average and spot reading modes is also a good way of checking if you are concerned about a potential exposure error. If there is a difference of more than about half a stop when using transparency film you need to consider the scene more carefully to decide if a degree of exposure compensation is required.

Technical Details

35mm SLR camera with a 75–300mm zoom lens and 81B warm-up filter on Fuji Velvia. ▼

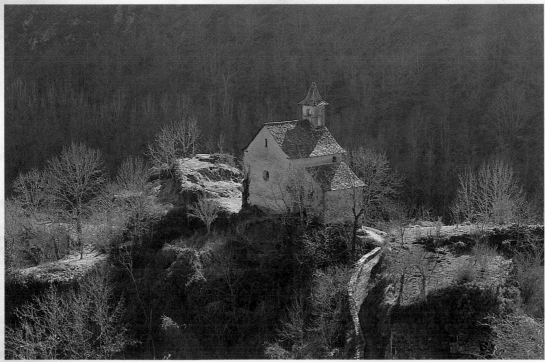

Near Conques in the Lot region of France

I gave two-thirds of a stop less exposure than the meter indicated for this image as the large area of darker tone suggested more exposure than was needed, which would have resulted in the lighter details of the image being too light.

Choosing Film

There is a huge variety of film types and speeds from which to choose and although, to a degree, it is dependent on personal taste there are some basic considerations to be made. Unless you wish to achieve special effects through the use of film grain it is generally best to choose a slow, fine-grained film for landscape photography if the subject and lighting conditions will permit.

The choice between colour negative film and transparency film depends partly upon the intended use of the photographs. For book and magazine reproduction transparency film is universally preferred and transparencies are also demanded by most photo libraries. For personal use, and when colour prints are the main requirement, colour negative film can be a better choice since it has greater exposure latitude and is capable of producing high-quality prints at a lower cost.

Although colour film is very widely used in landscape photography there are many qualities in such subjects which can also be used to produce striking black and white images. In addition to conventional black-and-white films like Ilford's FP4 and Kodak's Tri X there are also films such as Ilford's XP2 and Kodak's T400 CN which use colour negative technology and can be processed in the same way at one-hour photo labs to produce a monochrome print.

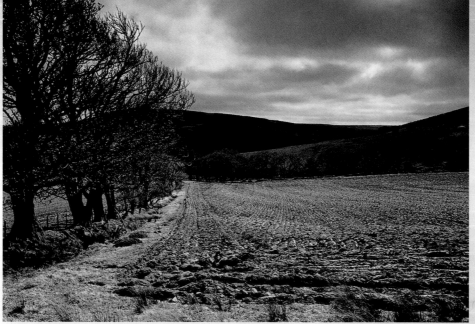

Technical Details
6 x 4.5cm SLR camera with a 55–110 mm zoom lens on Ilford's XP2.

Near Alnwick in Northumbria, UK

The rich tones and textures in this scene made it a good subject for black and white film. The additional control available when making a print in the darkroom enabled me to increase the contrast, print in the sky and hold back detail in some of the darker tones.

Black-and-white infrared film can be very effective for landscape photography when exposed through a red filter. This film is very sensitive and needs to be loaded and unloaded into the camera in very subdued light – a darkroom is best.

For those who like to experiment and produce images with a surreal quality, it can be interesting to use infrared film available in both black and white and colour transparency versions to create images with a most unusual range of tones and colours.

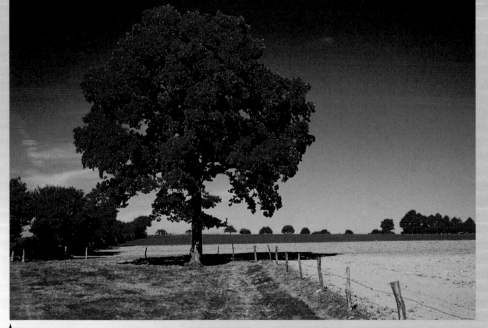

Near Honfleur in the Normandy region of France

This photograph was taken on Kodak's Infrared Ektachrome using the recommended yellow filter, a Wratten 12. The effects of this film are hard to predict and are dependent upon the subject, the filter used and the exposure. It is best to bracket exposures quite widely, based on an ISO rating of 200. I have had very interesting results using tobacco and sepia coloured filters. The film can be cross-processed in C41 chemistry to produce a negative from which even more unusual effects can be obtained.

Technical Details
35mm SLR camera with a 35–70mm zoom lens and a Wratten 12 filter on Kodak's Infrared Ektachrome.

Even in the best conditions, filters are essential, especially when shooting on colour transparency film, as even the brightest sunny day with the clearest blue sky and whitest of fluffy clouds can reproduce disappointingly unless every effort is made to get the very best from a scene.

Technique

A polarising filter is, perhaps, the most useful filter of all as it can influence the colours in a scene selectively and does not alter the overall colour balance of the image. It is equally effective when used with colour print film whereas the qualities created by a warm-up or neutral-graduated filter can be achieved when making colour prints from negatives.

While a polarising filter is mainly used for making blue skies a deeper colour with white clouds standing out in stronger relief they can have a much wider use than this. On overcast days they will often increase the colour saturation of foliage quite dramatically and produce much richer images – the effect on spring or autumn colours can be very striking.

A polarising filter can also help to give greater clarity when shooting distant views and is very useful for subduing excessively bright highlights when shooting into the light, like the sparkle on rippled water. Polarising filters need between one-and-a-half and two stops extra exposure but this will be allowed for automatically when using TTL metering.

Warm-up filters are essential to photographers shooting outdoors on colour transparency film as the colour temperature of daylight can increase far beyond that for which daylight film is balanced, especially on overcast or hazy days and beneath a deep blue sky, when a pronounced blue cast will be created.

Technical Details

35mm SLR camera with a 35–70mm zoom lens, 81C warm-up and polarising filters on Fuji Velvia.

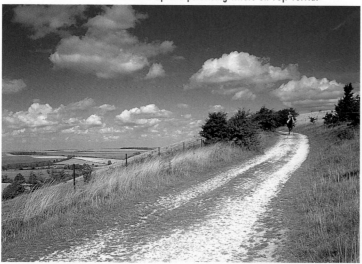

Win Green near Shaftesbury in Wiltshire, UK

I used a polarising filter to help create the striking relief of the white clouds in this scene and to increase the colour saturation of the blue sky.

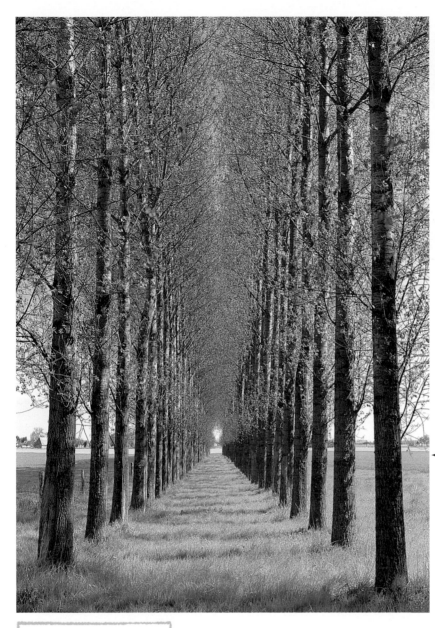

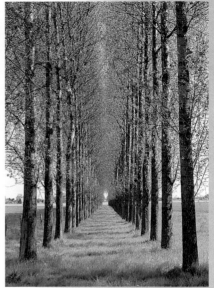

Near Rouen in the Normandy region of France

These two photographs show how the addition of filters affects the colour and quality of the image. The image on the left was taken with 81C warm-up and polarising filters while the one on the right was shot without the benefit of any filters.

◄**Technical Details**
35mm SLR camera with a 35–70mm zoom lens, 81C warm-up and polarising filters on Fuji Velvia.

Rule of Thumb

Neutral-graduated filters provide a very effective means of making the sky darker and revealing richer tones and colours. They can also reduce the contrast between a bright sky and a darker foreground, giving improved tones and colours in both. In addition, you can sometimes use a neutral-graduated filter effectively upside down to make a foreground darker.

Photographs For Pleasure & Profit

For most enthusiasts, the satisfaction of spending time in beautiful gardens and producing good photographs of them is a pleasure in itself, but it need only be the beginning of the benefits which this pursuit can bring.

Captioning

While a good photograph needs little further justification, images of subjects like gardens, plants and flowers can be given considerably greater interest and pleasure if the details of the photographs are recorded. And, of course, if you have ambitions to see your work in print, it is vital that your pictures are captioned accurately and filed efficiently.

The name and location of the garden is usually the prime category for photographs which have identifiable features, while for photographs of individual plants it can be useful to record the Latin name as well as its more common title, especially if you wish to submit photographs for publication.

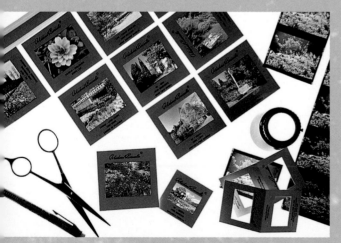

A light box, a powerful magnifying glass and a pair of sharp scissors are vital accessories for editing and mounting colour transparencies. The photograph shows pre-printed card mounts and caption labels protected by acetate sleeves and filed in a viewpack with a suspension bar for storage in a filing cabinet.

Storing your Pictures

Card mounts are by far the most suitable way of storing and presenting colour transparencies. They can be printed with your name and address together with caption information. Added protection can be given by the use of individual clear plastic sleeves which slip over the mount.

The simplest way of storing mounted transparencies is in viewpacks – large plastic sleeves with individual pockets which can hold up to 24 35mm slides or 15 120 transparencies. These can be fitted with bars for suspension in a filing-cabinet drawer and quickly and easily lifted out for viewing. For slide projection, however, it is far safer to use plastic mounts, preferably with glass covers, to avoid the risk of popping and jamming inside the projector.

Presentation

When colour transparencies are to be used as part of a portfolio, a more stylish and polished presentation can be created by using large black cut-out mounts which hold up to 20 or more slides in individual black mounts, depending upon format. These can be slipped into a protective plastic sleeve with a frosted back for easy viewing.

Prints, whether black-and-white or colour, are most effectively presented either individually or perhaps with two or three compatible images mounted on a page in a portfolio. This can be in book form or as individual mounts in a case or box. For added protection it is possible to have prints laminated.

Editing

When selecting work for any form of professional presentation you must be very critical of your pictures. Transparencies need to be spot on for exposure and pin sharp – use a light box and a powerful magnifier to eliminate any which are sub-standard.

It is also best to be quite ruthless about eliminating any rather similar or repetitive images. Even for personal use the impact of your photographs will be greatly increased if only the very best of each situation is included and a conscious effort is made to vary the nature of the pictures.

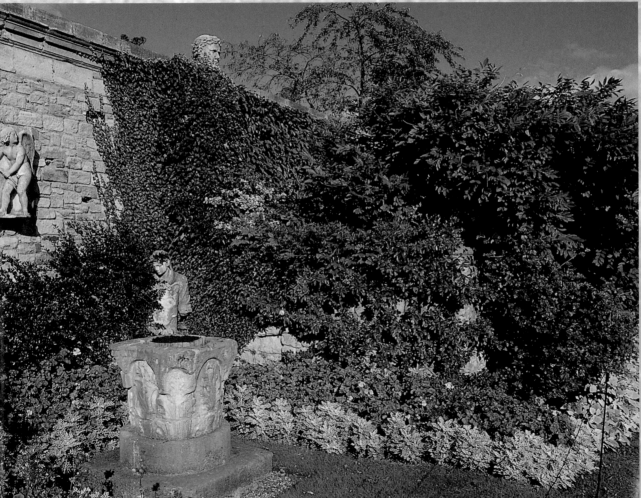

I have captioned this picture in the following way for my files:
'Hever Castle Gardens, near Edenbridge, Kent, UK... Italian garden in autumn with statues and ornaments, cinerarias and zonal pelargoniums.'

Glossary

Aperture priority

An auto-exposure setting in which the
user selects the aperture and the
camera's exposure system sets
the appropriate shutter speed.

APO lens

A highly-corrected lens which is
designed to give optimum definition
at wide apertures and is most often
available in the better-quality long-
focus lenses.

Ariel perspective

The tendency of distant objects to
appear bluer and lighter than close
details, enhancing the impression
of depth and distance in an image.

Auto-bracketing

A facility available on many cameras
which allows three or more exposures
to be taken automatically in quick
succession, giving both more and less
than the calculated exposure. This is
usually adjustable in increments of
one-third, half or one stop settings
and is especially useful when
shooting colour transparency film.

Bellows unit

An adjustable device which allows the
lens to be extended from the camera
body to focus at very close distances.

Cable release

A flexible device which attaches to the
camera's shutter-release mechanism
and which allows the shutter to be
fired without touching the camera.

Colour cast

A variation in a colour photograph from
the true colour of a subject which is
caused by the light source having a
different colour temperature to that
for which the film is balanced.

Colour temperature

A means of expressing the specific
colour quality of a light source in
degrees Kelvin (K). Daylight colour film
is balanced to give accurate colours at
around 5,600 degrees K but daylight
can vary from only 3,500 degrees K
close to sundown to over 20,000
degrees K in open shade when
there is a blue sky.

Cross processing

The technique of processing colour transparency film in colour negative chemistry, and vice versa, to obtain unusual effects.

Data back

A camera attachment which allows information like the time and date to be printed on the film alongside or within the images.

Dedicated flash

A flash gun which connects to the camera's metering system and controls the power of the flash to produce a correct exposure. It will also work when the flash is bounced or diffused.

Depth of field

The distance in front and behind the point at which a lens is focused which will be rendered acceptably sharp. It increases when the aperture is made smaller and extends about two-thirds behind the point of focus and one-third in front. The depth of field becomes smaller when the lens is focused at close distances. A scale indicating depth of field for each aperture is marked on most lens mounts and it can also be judged visually on SLR cameras which have a depth-of-field preview button.

DX coding

A system whereby a 35mm camera reads the film speed from a bar code printed on the cassette and sets it automatically.

Evaluative metering

An exposure meter setting in which brightness levels are measured from various segments of the image and the results used to compute an average. It's designed to reduce the risk of under or overexposing subjects with an abnormal tonal range.

Exposure compensation

A setting which can be used to give less or more exposure when using the camera's auto-exposure system for subjects which have an abnormal tonal range. It is usually adjustable in one-third of a stop increments.

Exposure latitude

The ability of a film to produce an acceptable image when an incorrect exposure is given. Negative films have a significantly greater exposure latitude than transparency films.

Extension tubes

Tubes of varying lengths which can be fitted between the camera body and lens to allow it to focus at close distances. These are usually available in sets of three different widths.

Fill-in flash

A camera setting for use with dedicated flash guns which controls the light output from a flash unit and allows it to be balanced with the subject's ambient lighting when it is too contrasty or there are deep shadows.

Filter factor

The amount by which the exposure must be increased to allow for the use of a filter. A x2 filter requires an increase of one stop and a x4 filter requires a two stop exposure increase.

Grey card

A piece of card which is tinted to reflect 18 per cent of the light falling upon it. It is the standard tone to which exposure meters are calibrated and can be used for substitute exposure readings when the subject is very light or dark in tone.

Hyperfocal distance

The closest distance at which details will be rendered sharp when the lens is focused on infinity. By focusing on the hyperfocal distance you can make maximum use of the depth of field at a given aperture.

Incident light reading

A method involving the use of a hand meter to measure the light falling upon a subject instead of that which is reflected from it.

ISO rating

The standard by which film speeds are measured. Most films fall within the range of ISO 25 to ISO 3200. A film with double the ISO rating needs one stop less exposure and a film with half the ISO rating needs one stop more exposure. The rating is subdivided into one-third of a stop settings i.e. 50, 64, 80, 100 and so on.

Macro lens

A lens which is designed to focus at close distances to give up to a life-size image of a subject.

Matrix metering

See evaluative metering.

Mirror lock

A device which allows the mirror of an SLR camera to be flipped up before the exposure is made to reduce vibration and avoid loss of sharpness when shooting close-ups or using a long-focus lens.

Polarising filter

A neutral grey filter which can reduce the brightness of reflections on non-metallic surfaces such as water, foliage and blue sky.

Programmed exposure

An auto-exposure setting in which the camera's metering system sets both aperture and shutter speed according the subject matter and lighting conditions. It usually offers choices like landscape, close-up, portrait, action etc.

Pulling

A means of lowering the stated speed of a film by reducing the development times.

Pushing

A means of increasing the stated speed of a film by increasing the development times.

Reciprocity failure

The effect when very long exposures are given. Some films become effectively slower when exposures of more than one second are given and doubling the length of the exposure does not have as much effect as opening up the aperture by one stop.

Shutter priority

A setting on auto-exposure cameras which allows the photographer to set the shutter speed while the camera's metering system selects the appropriate aperture.

Spot metering

A means of measuring the exposure from a small and precise area of the image which is often an option on SLR cameras. It is useful when calculating the exposure from high-contrast subjects or those with an abnormal tonal range.

Substitute reading

An exposure reading taken from an object of average tone which is illuminated in the same way as the subject. This is a useful way of calculating the exposure for a subject which is much lighter or darker than average.